FINDING RODA ANNE

Bert Goolsby

Finding Roda Anne

Finding Roda Anne

Copyright © 2014 Bert Goolsby
Cover Art Copyright © 2014 Karen Michelle Nutt
Edited by Megan Leonard
Design Consultant and Formatting Laura Shinn
2d Edition

Licensing Notes
All rights reserved under U.S. and International copyright law. This ARC is licensed only for the private use of the reviewer or for the author to use as contest and promotional prizes. May not be copied, scanned, digitally reproduced, or printed for re-sale, may not be uploaded on shareware or free sites, or used in any other manner without the express written permission of the author and/or publisher. Thank you for respecting the hard work of the author.

Finding Roda Anne is a work of fiction. Though actual locations may be mentioned, they are used in a fictitious manner and the events and occurrences were invented in the mind and imagination of the author except for the inclusion of actual historical facts. Similarities of characters or names used within to any person – past, present, or future – are coincidental except where actual historical characters are purposely interwoven.

Bert Goolsby

Dedication

In memory of my late brother Thomas Cowart Goolsby.

Finding Roda Anne

Acknowledgments

I am grateful to those who read the manuscript and offered me their suggestions: Fred Alexander, Cindy Robertson, Jim Ellisor, my wife Prue, and, of course, the Inkplots Writing Group.

Bert Goolsby

OTHER TITLES

Fiction

The Locusts of Padgett County

The Trials of Lawyer Pratt

Familiar Shadows

Five Stockings

Harpers' Joy

On Grandma's Porch (anthology with various authors)

More Sweet Tea (anthology with various authors)

Humanity, Darling

Her Own Law

The Box with the Green Bow and Ribbon

Sweet Potato Biscuits and Other Stories

Nonfiction

Lex Christi

90 Daily Devotions for Lawyers & Judges and Those They Serve

The South Carolina Tort Claims Act: A Primer and Then Some

Finding Roda Anne

CHAPTER ONE

Lawyers sweat. I'm a lawyer. So I sweat. I sweat attracting work. I sweat doing the work once I get it, and I sweat getting paid for the work once I've done it.

And I sweat because I practice law in a place way down in the really Deep South where they say the only thing that separates its summer heat from the heat of Hell is a screen door. Some days the humidity down here gets so high, folks can almost swim in the air.

Yet I do try to take advantage of the heat. On the days when it gets so hot folks can hardly breathe, I make it a point to hand out a dipper full of ice-cold water to anyone who comes traipsing by my law office. Why do I do it? I've found it's a durn good way for me to become acquainted with potential jurors and to grab a new client now and then, that's how come.

I say my "law office." It's not a law office like most people would probably picture—you know, an office on the second floor of a downtown bank building furnished with mahogany furniture, oriental rugs, fancy lamps, and law books, and with diplomas and certificates and all kinds of framed art hung on its walls. No, mine is more like what they used to call a "rolling store," only mine's a "rolling office." By that I mean it's an office that's got four tires under it, each one a recap.

Right after I got admitted to the Bar, I went looking for a law office. But everything I looked at near the courthouse proved to be way too expensive for me, starting out like I was with only the little bit of money I'd saved from playing in dance bands when I was in college and law school and from sacking groceries at a supermarket while waiting to hear back from the bar examiners.

I'd about given up on finding an office I could afford when the milkman who serviced the supermarket told me about this 1949 Divco truck for sale by his company, the East End Dairy Company. They put it up for sale when they'd decided to quit home milk delivery. I got it at a pretty good price.

Being good with my hands, I converted it into a law office. Billy Joe Pratt, my best friend and seatmate at law school and, like me, a two-time candidate for the Bar, helped me do it, although he didn't do too much. About the only thing he's good at is running his mouth, but I don't reckon that's a bad thing for a lawyer or, for that matter, a preacher or a salesman either.

One other thing about Billy Joe, he's got what he calls a "float-qualified" secretary, Dixie St. John. She's not only as beautiful as all get-out—and Billy Joe wouldn't admit this in a million years—she's savvy and quick-witted, too. There's no telling how many clients Billy Joe has attracted since she went to work for him. I know this: she's a whole lot better "draw" than a dipper of ice-cold water, no question about it.

But getting back to the truck, Billy Joe and I added a matching leather passenger seat to the cab to go with the one used by the driver and installed a pocket door to close the partition between the cab and rear cargo area. We finished the cargo area by adding interior walls made of light-colored wood paneling and by laying down dark-blue, wall-to-wall carpet on the floor.

For office furnishings, we bolted a desk, a filing cabinet, and two chairs to the floorboard and built in a glass-enclosed bookcase. We screwed down "in" and "out" trays to the desktop and stored my portable Underwood typewriter and a few other office things in the bottom of the file cabinet. We put the bookcase in mostly for appearances because it only held a few law books—mainly textbooks from my law school days and a formbook.

To give my office a professional look, I framed and hung my law school and undergraduate diplomas, bar admission certificate, and notary commission. When Billy

Joe and I got it all finished, everything looked right nice, even if I do say so myself.

I didn't neglect the exterior of the truck. I paid to have it painted purple—the color that stands for the law—and got a sign painter to print on both sides and the rear of the truck in large, black letters my name "Deloris Meek, Esquire", and the words "Lawyer" and "Notary Public." I also had him add a line—one I came up with all by myself—that read, "Let me press your suit"; but the local Bar Association complained to the Lawyer Grievance Commission about it, and they made me paint over it. They said it amounted to unlawful solicitation, a no-no under the Code of Ethics for Lawyers. For a while there, I feared they might try to disbar me. I suppose they took into account I really didn't know any better and that's why they took pity on me.

I got lucky on a permanent place to park my "office" whenever I wasn't out following an ambulance or a wrecker or cruising around in it to advertise myself. Kingry Insurance, a general insurance agency that sat next door to the courthouse, provided homeowner insurance coverage to the first person I sued. It was an action for what I called "yard defilement." My client's next-door neighbor's dog kept memorializing his visits, if you know what I mean. I know the suit was what Billy Joe called a "pea-in-the-shoe" type of thing—one that's more of an aggravation than anything else—but the insurance company settled the case anyway, thank the good Lord. Talk about sweating, I really sweated that one out, I tell you.

As part of the deal, I got Kingry Insurance to agree to rent me three parking spaces in return for my promising I'd never sue any of their customers ever again. Also, they gave me access to one line of their telephone and to one of their secretaries whenever I needed either. Of course, I had to pay for long-distance calls—and for secretary time too, which was all right with me since I used the "hunt and peck, hit, miss, and erase" system of typing.

Like I said, on hot days during the summer months I usually sit outside my office and offer cold water to people who might happen to walk by. But what I'm about to tell you started late one afternoon in August 1965.

By then, I'd been a licensed lawyer for about three years. I remember the heat that day had gotten so bad that by mid-afternoon the fire ants were smearing themselves with suntan lotion. I'd spent most of the afternoon, with my coat off, trolling for clients as I sat in the shade of my truck, fanning myself with a cardboard paddle fan. Every time somebody came walking by, I'd yell out, while waving a dipper of cold water, "Hey, hot enough for you?"

Usually, folks would look my way when they heard me, and some would saunter over. I'd pour a little ice water into a paper cup, hand it to them along with my business card, and shoot the breeze while they gulped the water down. Most would thank me, slip the card into a pocket or purse, and walk on off. Others would engage in small talk for a moment or two. A lot of times, the conversations would end with them asking me for free legal advice, for directions, or for money. Once in a while, somebody'd ask me, a Baptist, if I was saved. I always said I was, although, to be honest about it, I never was quite sure I was because I played in dance bands from time to time and Baptists, so I'd been taught, aren't supposed to believe in dancing—at least, dancing with girls—that is, if you are a boy.

Anyway, I decided to call it a day about 5:00 o'clock. All that heat and my fanning up a storm and getting up and down a million times to give ice water away finally got to me. I never was one for physical exertion, although I did play football in high school—I was a third-string fullback, nicknamed "Bartlett" by my teammates because of my pear-shaped body.

I often think my dislike of physical exercise is the main reason I took to the law rather than try to do something else. Its practice affords much in the way of what I call "sitting-down work" and entails little in the way of heavy lifting for lawyers and none at all for judges.

The afternoon, though, had not been a total failure. I picked up a couple of clients, one charged with driving under the influence and the other with running a red light. Each man, both textile workers, was guilty as sin, near as I could tell. But if they wanted to waste their money on a lawyer, who was I to argue? About all I could do for them would be to get them a continuance a time or two—you know, postpone the inevitable time when their "sins" would find them out.

After I decided to call it a day, I emptied out what remained of the water and ice, packed up the barrel, dipper, and cups, and threw everything into the back of the truck. Though I was Baptist-raised, I headed for the Rosewater Lounge, my usual after-hours haunt and, I might add, that of a few other Baptists as well, plus some other types of Christians and a lot of the unchurched. Those of us who frequented the place called it the "Poor man's country club."

The second I opened the door to the Rosewater I caught a whiff of the coldest beer in town and the sound of Loretta Lynn's new recording of "Blue Kentucky Girl." I could barely hear Loretta, though, the barroom laughter and chatter being what it was.

I dropped my big butt down onto the only seat available, a bar stool. I didn't realize until it was too late that I had sat down next to Eugene "Hack" Hackberry. He was always at the Rosewater, so much so you'd think he came with the lease. Hack had consumed so much beer over the years his ballooning belly made his arms stick out like little flippers.

Once I got served, I started looking around for a vacant seat either in a booth or on another stool near the back because I couldn't stand sitting next to Hack. He was always making up lawyer jokes and trying them out on me. Few, if any, of them ever struck me as funny, probably because, being rather new to the practice, I still held the Law as second only to the Bible in importance.

Hack grinned at me once he turned his head my way. "Why hello, Counselor," he said. "Caught you any ambulances lately?"

"Nope, sure haven't," I said with a grump. "They've got now where they can outrun me. Got them big engines, doncha know."

"Yeah?" Hack laughed. "Let you in on a little secret." He cupped a hand to his mouth and bent toward me. "The trick is to wait till they stop." Then he elbowed me and just laughed and laughed.

"Oh, I see," I said. "Wait till they stop, huh? Thanks. I'll try to remember that."

Hack poked me in the side again with his elbow, almost causing me to drop my beer. "I betcha didn't hear the one about this lawyer what falls dead and goes to Heaven, didcha?"

Without waiting for me to answer, Hack began telling me the story anyway. "He's real surprised to end up there, see." Hack paused to chuckle at himself. "So, he says to Saint Peter, *Look here, am I in the right place?* Saint Peter says to him, *Yeah. Well, at least for right now, you are. The Lord called down here a minute ago, said he wanted to see what an honest lawyer looked like, and he wanted to see one right now. Well, you just happened to be the best we could come up with on such short notice.* The lawyer says, *But I ain't honest.* Saint Peter says, *"We know you ain't, but you do have an honest look about you."*

I just rolled my eyes. I wasn't about to give him the satisfaction of a laugh.

Hack stared at me for a second. "See, the Lord didn't say he wanted to see an honest lawyer. No, he only wanted to see what one of them looked like. And so that's what they done, Saint Peter and them. They got one that *looked* like he was. Know what I'm saying?"

"Uh, huh," I said. "I get it now."

But I still didn't laugh.

The jukebox kicked in again, this time spinning Johnny Cash's latest hit, "Orange Blossom Special."

"Excuse me, sir," someone said. It came from a man seated two stools down. The man, who appeared hearse-ready, sported a white mustache, very nicely trimmed. "You a lawyer, I take it, sir? I heard you called 'Counselor' just now."

I swiveled around to my right and pointed to my chest. "You talking to me?"

"Yes. I couldn't help overhearing your conversation. I gather you practice law?"

"When I can, I do," I said.

The man strolled over and offered his hand. "I'm Colonel Loomis."

I drew back and scrutinized him a bit as we shook hands. "Colonel, huh? Retired Army?"

He shook his head. "No. Auctioneer. 'Colonel' is just an honorary title we auctioneers have."

"That so? Why's that?"

"Way I understand it, during the Civil War whenever soldiers went to divide up their plunder they'd have an auction, and only officers who were colonels or above could conduct the bidding process. That's how it started out."

The colonel gestured toward a booth that just became empty. "How about we sit over there, son, and let me buy you another beer."

Welcoming the chance to get away from Hack, I quickly agreed. The colonel and I hurried over to the booth before someone else could beat us to it.

"If you don't mind talking a little shop, I'd like to discuss a legal matter with you, Mr.—"

"Meek. Deloris Meek." I dug for my business card and handed it to Loomis.

The card read, "Deloris Meek, Esquire, Advocate for the Lame, the Halt, the Injured, the Wrongful Dead, the Accused, the Jailed, the Bailed, and the Catching Hell."

Loomis read the card, smiled, and pocketed it. "The 'Catching Hell,' huh?"

"Yes, sir," I said, with a nod. "Them especially."

"And if somebody wants to get in touch with you, the card says to dial the number for Kingry Insurance and ask for you. I gather you're in the insurance business too, Mr. Meek?"

"Not really. They just handle my phone calls."

"They do?" he said, sounding as if he didn't quite believe me.

"Yes, sir. That's part of a deal I've got with them. Long story."

"Tell me something. How about wills, you do them?"

I scratched my cheek. "Never have. But I'm game if you are. Took wills and estates in law school, though, and passed that section on the bar exam."

For the next forty minutes or so over a couple of beers, the colonel and I engaged first in some small talk, and then discussed how he wanted his property disposed of after his death. One thing he was dead set on: he wanted to leave everything he owned to some woman named "Roda Anne Harrison."

I asked him who she was, and all he would say right then was, "She is who she is, that's who."

Now that didn't tell me a thing. But if he wanted to leave it to Roda Anne Harrison or John Doe, I didn't care in the least. At least not right then, I didn't.

* * * * *

Since Colonel Loomis was in a big hurry to have his will prepared and it was a simple one to draft, I agreed to do him one overnight, get it typed, and meet him the following morning at his place to get it executed. He lived way out in the sticks on C.R. 819, an unpaved, often full-of-holes county road. He told me to turn into a private drive that lay by a mailbox topped with a small sign that read "Grind Stone." Much to my surprise, I found the drive without any trouble. Once on it, I drove about a quarter of a mile through a thick forest of twenty-something-year-old pines until I reached a clearing where a late model Chrysler and a rundown Ford pickup sat side by side.

About thirty yards from the clearing I spotted a brick walkway that led through some more pine trees. A huge, gray millstone lay at the end of the brick path. Beyond it and beneath a number of towering evergreens lay one of the most beautiful homes I'd ever seen. Four square columns stood on each side of the entranceway to the home, two supporting eaves above a small balcony and two supporting the balcony. A lawn of freshly mowed centipede surrounded the house, whose wood siding had been painted a soft white. A wide variety of shrubs and flowers, looking cozy with fresh pine straw packed all around them, enhanced the grass at almost every turn. On the right side of the house, a shaded screened porch equipped with green awnings reached out to a slew of ancient crepe myrtles.

I knocked on the door using its brass knocker. The colonel surprised me by answering the door himself. After seeing where he lived, I had expected somebody with a British accent and dressed in butler get-up to do that.

The colonel pushed open the screen door. "Well, good morning, big fella. Won't you come in? You got here a bit earlier than I expected you to."

I gulped as my face suddenly warmed. I remembered something Billy Joe told me his daddy told him one time. He said his daddy said, "Son, there's one thing what's worser than being late, and that's being early. The early bird might catch the worm, all right, but sometimes he might be better off if he hadn't've done it. That worm just might not sit too well with him."

I quickly apologized to the colonel for my early arrival and tried to justify it. "To tell the truth, Colonel, I didn't rightly know how long it might take me to find your place. Plus, I'm not too good at following directions, doncha know. When I played football in high school, my coach, he used to get real upset with me if I didn't run the right route whenever I got the ball. He told me one time he didn't think I could find my ass using a hand-held mirror, a blue-tick hound, and a board-certified proctologist pointing at it with a yard stick."

The colonel smiled as I stepped past him into the foyer. "Well, son, looks like you proved him wrong this time."

He nodded toward a well-lighted room off to his left. "Let's go in here, sir."

The room had two couches, a bunch of paintings, lots of old photographs, a big fireplace, several chairs and tables, and an opened bookcase loaded with leather-bound books that gave off a musty odor. He suggested I take a seat on one of the couches. I did, and he sat down in a high-back chair next to it.

I kept looking around the room after I took my seat. "I'll have to say this is just about the most beautiful house I think I've ever been in, Colonel. You build it, sir?"

"No, my late wife and her first husband, they did." He shrugged. "When she died, she left it to me."

Just as I was thinking well now, how lucky can you get, he added, "That's when I found out how appropriate they'd named the place. Grind Stone. It's a grindstone, all right. Takes damn near every cent I can lay my hands on to maintain it. I've been thinking of selling it." He crossed his legs and cupped his hands. "But enough about that. You have any trouble drafting the will, Mr. Meek?"

"Well, just a little bit, sir. Nothing I couldn't handle."

I didn't tell him I had adapted it from a formbook on wills that Billy Joe loaned me. The only trouble I had was running down Billy Joe to borrow the book.

"I hope I got it like you wanted it, sir."

I reached for my briefcase, opened it, and withdrew the will Mr. Kingry's secretary had typed for me early that morning. I looked around. "Colonel, we gotta have us three witnesses, doncha know—State law."

"Well, the man who kinda looks after the place for me, he's here. His name's Jay Wyndam. Fact, he and two other men are out back right this very minute doing some touch-up painting and replacing some flashing around one of the chimneys. How about them? Will they do?"

"Long as they can sign their name, can see to do it, and, as the saying goes, ain't crazy as a possum in a privy."

The colonel laughed. "Oh, they'll be all right. I better tell you, though, I understand one of them—the one called 'Turbyfill'—he's a little slow and he's been in and out of trouble, mainly alcohol-related offenses, such as public drunk. I don't think he's been arrested for anything serious. Otherwise, I don't think Jay would put up with him, and I certainly wouldn't want him around here if he's a thief or violent. Jay knows that."

The colonel rocked himself forward in an effort to stand. "Sit right there while I call them inside."

"You might better read what I drafted first, doncha know. If it's not right, I'll have to beat it back to town and get it retyped. And while I'm at it, I could get us some other witnesses, if you want me to." I was thinking of asking Billy Joe, his secretary, and investigator.

Colonel Loomis settled back in his chair as I handed him the blue-backed document.

It took him less than two minutes to read the will. When he finished, he laid it down on his lap and sat there, looking off to the side for a little bit. He exhaled some air and said to me, "Thank you, Mr. Meek. It's fine, really."

I was relieved to hear that.

"But there is one thing."

My heart skipped a beat. I just knew something had to be wrong with it. I seldom do anything right, it seems.

"You left blank the name of my executor," he said.

"Yes, sir. You didn't tell me who you wanted, and I forgot to ask you about that. We can fill it in when you get ready to sign it, doncha know. That won't be no problem doing that. Just write in the name you want and initial it. And we'll get the witnesses to initial it, too, just to be on the safe side. I asked Billy Joe Pratt about that—he's another lawyer—and he said we could do it thataway."

The colonel pressed his lips together and stared off to the side again. "How about this, sir. Would you agree to be my executor?"

That got my attention, so much so that I lost my breath for a second or two. "But Colonel," I managed to say, "you don't know nothing about me, nothing at all."

"You are a licensed lawyer, and I hear you give away free ice water. Also, Doc tells me you're a good man." The colonel was referring to Doc Eleazer, a retired chiropractor who owned and operated the Rosewater.

I didn't know what else to say and told the colonel that.

"And if you turn out to be a bad choice, I won't know anything about it, now will I?" the colonel said. "So, what the hell. How about it? You willing to do that for me?

And I'd want you to serve as the lawyer for the estate as well. You could pay yourself the going rate, both as the Estate's executor and as its lawyer."

I stood and offered the colonel my hand. "Colonel, sir, I'd be honored to do it, if that's whatcha really, really want."

He stood, took my hand, and shook it, after which we both sat back down.

"But one thing I'd appreciate if you'd do for me," I said.

"What's that?"

"I'd need an up-to-date list of your assets and liabilities and the name of your bank and where the key to your safety deposit box is, if you've got one. Your house key, too, come to think of it. And it'd help to have a listing of all your next-of-kin and their addresses and phone numbers. I know you're leaving everything to that one lady, but just in case—certainly her address."

He nodded. "Anything else?"

"I can't think of nothing else. Oh yeah. Maybe whatcha funeral plans are. I'd probably need to know all about them, unless you've already made some arrangements."

He shook his head. "Not yet, I haven't. I mean, I haven't pre-arranged things with any particular funeral home. But I did write down which one to take my body to and what I want done and all after I'm dead. I've put the instructions in an envelope in the top drawer of that secretary right over there," he said, indicating. "I don't want much—you know, in the way of frills. No sense spending a bunch of money on somebody who can't appreciate it."

I nodded my agreement, as if it were really any of my business what he wanted his money to go for after he was dead and gone.

"If there's nothing else, I reckon, you can ask your witnesses to join us."

Finding Roda Anne

Colonel Loomis stood. "I'll be right back."

While I waited on him to return with his witnesses, I tried to think of some other things I might need from him; but I couldn't think of anything else right then. I also wondered if I'd have any trouble finding Roda Anne Harrison, whoever she was. With any luck, I would hope to complete the administration of the colonel's estate within six months and pick up some easy money.

The estate seemed simple enough, what with only one heiress to mess with and the colonel's promising to get me all the addresses I'd need and a list of all his assets and liabilities. Basically, about the only thing I'd have to do is contact the funeral home, get in touch with the Harrison woman, pay some bills, and fill out a bunch of forms, which the probate judge would even help me to do.

Then, all of a sudden, I remembered what this old law professor once told us about handling decedent estates. He said, "Be careful when you agree to handle one. You never know where it might take you, and that's because, when you're dealing with the dead, they're not in a position to tell you a damn thing."

CHAPTER TWO

Less than two weeks after the colonel executed his will I got a call from his yardman telling me the colonel had dropped dead behind his house in a grassy spot between the water tower and the horse stables.

The first thing I did was call Billy Joe Pratt. I didn't know what needed to be done right then. The only time I ever had anything to do with dead folks was when my daddy died, but I was a little boy then and Mama took care of everything.

Billy Joe drove with me out to Grind Stone. When we neared the drive, a hearse pulled out onto the road and headed toward town. Once we reached the house, we found the yardman and his helper standing out front with the coroner. They took us to the spot on the back lawn where they'd found the colonel and showed it to us.

Talking to the coroner, we learned the colonel had been out watering some flowers. The coroner said he must've just keeled over and probably died of a heart attack. He'd been dead, the coroner estimated, for less than an hour when the yardman just happened to find him, lying there on the ground with the water still scooting out of the hose at some red geraniums.

Billy Joe and I went on inside the house, the back door being left unlocked. When we walked into the kitchen, I spied a pot of coffee on the stove and an open sack of coffee on the counter. Billy Joe sniffed the air and remarked on the inviting aroma of the coffee and asked me if it'd be all right for him to have a cup. I told him to go ahead, that I didn't want any myself, and, besides, I wouldn't even think about drinking a dead man's coffee.

Billy Joe just laughed and said, "Lemme understand this, Deloris. You won't drink the man's coffee, but you'll take his money. Is that right?"

I didn't answer him. I felt like he was being disrespectful of the dead. What's more, I wasn't taking the colonel's money. I'd be earning it.

We found the will, a set of house keys, and other stuff without any trouble. They were just where the colonel said I'd find everything—in the top drawer of the secretary.

I opened the envelope on which he'd written "Funeral Plans" first thing. I discovered I had me a problem right off. The colonel said he wanted his body handled by Baxley Stokes Funeral Home. But now Harter Brothers Funeral Home had it. The coroner, without asking anybody, had called them to come get it. I asked Billy Joe what I ought to do—whether I should try to get the body sent over to Baxley Stokes or not. All Billy Joe said was, "My daddy always said, *When in doubt, do nothing.* Anyway, what difference will it make to the colonel? He's dead. He's not gonna know any better."

So, I did nothing—nothing, that is, about transferring the body to the other funeral home.

Later that same day, though, after I had filed the will and the probate judge had granted my application to be appointed the colonel's executor, I drove over to Harter Brothers Funeral Home and met with the two brothers, Lawrie and Ira. I showed them the instructions the colonel had left. They didn't think much of them and started pressuring me to add other services and things, saying the colonel must not have been thinking straight when he wrote all those down.

One item they kept insisting on that I buy was a vault. Since the colonel's instructions didn't say anything at all about a vault, I took the omission to mean he didn't want one. So, I didn't authorize it. I did buy him a coffin, of course, but it was the cheapest one they had—just like the colonel wanted me to. Billy Joe, who went with me to the funeral home, told me the coffin, which was little more than a wooden box, looked used.

In addition to the coffin, I had to buy some other services, such as opening and closing the grave, directing the funeral, and the like. I also bought a headstone from Memory Marble and Granite and instructed them to inscribe below the dates of his birth and death and his full name and honorary title, an epitaph I came up with all by myself. It read, "Bids closed. Soul to Christ Jesus." Being he'd been an auctioneer, I also told them to carve in a little gavel under the epitaph. Billy Joe suggested that could be kinda misleading because someone might think Colonel Loomis had been something other than an auctioneer. "You know, the president of the Civitans or a justice of the peace or something like that," he said.

The last thing I did to get ready for the colonel's funeral was to get in touch with his preacher, Brother Billy Arnot. I learned from the Harters that Brother Arnot, when he wasn't working the morning shift at the local hosiery mill, served as pastor or, as he dubbed his position, "preacher and revelator" of the Mount Olive Evangelical Tabernacle Church, Reformed—a congregation Billy Joe would probably describe as "anti-fundamentalist." By that he'd meant they stood four-square against anything "fun and mental."

I have to say the colonel's choice of preachers and church affiliation surprised me. Considering his wealth and where I'd first run into him, I had figured him a "high-church" man and not some kinda Bible-buster.

The good reverend and I agreed to meet in the break room at his workplace. When I walked into the room, I caught him rocking the drink machine back and forth and shouting curses at it. On seeing me, he laughed and said. "It seems, Mr. Meek, the sin of thievery ain't limited to human beings. Ol' Satan, he's done made this machine here steal my ten cents. And like the blessed Jesus done one time to this here fig tree what didn't have no fruit on it, I done laid a curse on it. That'll learn it. They'll never get it to work now."

Brother Arnot impressed me as an energetic little fellow. The whole time the two of us talked, he was bouncing and twisting around whether standing or sitting, a worn Bible in his hand. Like me, he had light skin and thinning red hair. Unlike me, though, his hair had started to turn gray. Also, he had light blue eyes whereas mine are green. Almost every other sentence he uttered ended, it seemed like, with an "amen."

I told him about the colonel's wish to have a simple funeral and asked him to contact Harter Brothers regarding the arrangements and everything.

When I stood to leave, he grabbed my arm and said, "Mr. Meek, I usually get twenty-five dollars—in advance."

"What?" I said.

He dropped his head. "It's kinda a love offering, you know. Amen."

I opened my wallet and withdrew twenty-five dollars. He counted along as I peeled off one ten-dollar bill, two fives, and five ones and laid them into his outstretched hand.

He then closed his eyes, nodded, and said, "Thank you, Jesus. Amen and amen."

I didn't mind his thanking Jesus for the money, but I felt like he owed some thanks to the colonel too. After all, that's who I'd be hitting for a reimbursement.

* * * * *

In any case, I was beginning to feel pretty good about all I had done in carrying out the colonel's funeral instructions; but before I could rest on my laurels, I got a phone call the morning after the colonel's death from this real hateful-talking woman. She claimed she was the colonel's niece by marriage and identified herself as Bessie

Phillips. She said she'd heard about the colonel's passing. She went on to say she and her two brothers had just come from the probate judge's office where they had tried to get one of them appointed the estate's representative. That's when they found out I'd already been named executor under the colonel's last will and testament.

    The woman said they asked to read the will and got bowled over when they learned the colonel left everything he owned to the Harrison woman, somebody they'd never heard of before. After seeing what was in the will, they then went and talked to one of the Harter brothers and later to Brother Arnot.

    She told me in no uncertain terms they didn't like the way I was handling the colonel's funeral arrangements and I had better get their uncle a vault and a better casket and get her and her brothers and the preacher a limousine for them to ride back and forth in to the funeral and cemetery or else. She went on to say they'd already talked about bringing legal action against the estate and me as well as turning me in to the Lawyer Grievance Committee for practicing fraud and using undue influence on their uncle. She and her brothers thought it very odd, she said, that their uncle didn't leave them "one red cent" as good as they'd been to him and all, and that they couldn't imagine his leaving everything to somebody they'd never heard of before, "not once." Then she said, "There's some hanky-panky going on here, I just know there is. I want you to know that me and my brothers, we weren't born yesterday."

    When I tried to explain to her I was just doing what the colonel wanted me to do, she said I was just like all lawyers and called me a "low-down, lying dog" and another name I had to look up in my dictionary—a "fabulist," a word she preceded with another "F" word, which I immediately understood.

    "Fine Christian talk," I told her just before hanging up on her.

After mulling over what'd happened, I called Billy Joe to tell him about Bessie Phillips' phone call and what she'd said. I told him her threat to turn me into the grievance committee if I didn't do what they wanted me to do troubled me the most. He said, "Aw, Deloris, I wouldn't let that worry me none."

"Well, I don't reckon you would," I said. "You're not the one they're threatening to turn in."

* * * * *

The next day I dropped by Billy Joe's office to see if he and his secretary might wanna go to Colonel Loomis' funeral with me. I found the two of them together in Billy Joe's outer office with him holding a cup of coffee while attempting to regale her with a "war story" about a magistrate's court trial he'd lucked out and won the day before.

Dixie came across as being bored half to tears, sitting there in front of her typewriter with her head down, her mouth opened, and her eyes half-closed. Near as I could tell, the case didn't amount to a hill of beans, involving a charge against Billy Joe's client of hunting doves over a baited field.

When I told Billy Joe what I wanted, he looked at me like he'd seen a monkey doing a crossword puzzle. "You gotta be kidding me, Deloris. He ain't my client. He's yours."

"Don't look at me," Dixie said, awake now and twirling two sheets of typing paper separated by one of carbon paper into her typewriter. "I don't do funerals. Besides, I've work to do." She angled her head toward Billy Joe. "Unlike him."

Her remark made Billy Joe laugh and say, "You got work to do? That's news to me."

She put her hands to her hips, pressed her lips together, and gave him a hard look. "What was that you said?"

Billy Joe couldn't apologize fast enough. "All I meant was I didn't know you still had some work to do," he said in a voice that could've belonged to a misbehaving sissy. Although he tried to throw his weight around with Dixie from time to time—telling her what to do and what she couldn't—she had his number. Truth to tell, she was so pretty she could control most any man.

So, I went to the funeral all by my lonesome, dreading it and, like most everybody else there, feeling glad it wasn't me at the center of attention right then.

The church building wasn't very large. It was constructed of unpainted cement blocks, roofed with white, mildew-streaked shingles, and fitted with a set of red-painted double doors that opened onto a tiny stoop out front. Each side of the building had three frosty-glass windows. The church lacked both shrubs and grass, although three large sweet gum trees stood out front, dropping their brown spiked balls everywhere. A small cross rose from the top of the building. But the church's most attention-getting items were a sign and an enclosure. The sign, the size of a billboard, advertised the name of the church and, just below it in larger letters, that of the preacher. The sign stood close to the highway, rising just inside a ten-foot-high cyclone fence that surrounded the church grounds and parking area. The gate to the entrance featured two much smaller signs, one reading "No Trespassing" and the other reading "The Lord Will Forgive Trespassers but the Law Won't."

When I went inside the church, I recognized a few people from the Rosewater, including Doc Eleazer. I would've tried to sit with him, except Hack Hackberry was beside him. I didn't feel like hearing any of Hack's stupid lawyer jokes.

As it turned out, I couldn't have sat with Doc anyway because the moment I entered the church Lawrie Harter motioned for me to follow him down front. He parked me on the first pew, right next to the colonel's yard man whose body odor signaled he'd failed, as they say, to "Mum-up" that morning—either he forgot to apply the deodorant, or he didn't use the stuff to start with, probably the latter. On his other side sat this long-necked, tallow-faced, middle-aged woman and these two big-eyed, long-necked, long-faced, versions of the woman. The latter wore rumpled black suits and gray vests and tan shoes. The two men reminded me of Heckle and Jeckle, these two cartoon magpies. Although I didn't recognize them, I figured the woman, since she was sitting on the front row, was the one who had called and threatened me the day before.

After the undertakers rolled the coffin in, they parked it in front of the pulpit and propped the lid open. I could make out the colonel's nose and a little bit of his hair from where I sat. No sooner had the undertakers turned to walk back up the aisle than the woman started carrying on something awful. If I hadn't known any better, I would have sworn somebody was touching her with a red-hot fire poker, the way she acted, squalling and all. I looked at the two men. Their bodies began jerking and shaking and each one's head started bobbing up and down like a paddleball being hit over and over again.

All of a sudden, the woman flung herself onto the floor and started flopping and rolling all about. Then she screamed, "Colonel, why'd you go and die? Why? Why? Why? I can't stand this. Oh, Jesus! Why couldn't it've been me?"

After that, she crawled on all fours over to the casket where she grabbed hold of the accordion-like framework beneath, shaking it back and forth and bawling all the while. I thought for a moment, she was going to topple the casket over on top of her. As it was, she shook loose some of the roses in the flower blanket that lay on the casket. They fell to the floor, and one got tangled in her hair.

She probably would have gone on like this until the service started had Ira Harter not come running down the aisle and start fanning her. Finally, one of the magpies put an arm under her, lifted her back onto the pew, and held her close, tears flooding down his face. A moment or so later, she calmed down to the point where she would just sniffle every now and then and mumble something I couldn't quite make out. She cut her eyes at me once or twice, probably to see if I was looking at her so I would notice how hard she was taking it.

The service began when Brother Arnot, his chin held high and his eyes closed tight, suddenly appeared to the right of the pulpit. He'd been sitting behind it all this time, hidden from sight. Over to the left sat the choir, four women and a man, each one decked out in a white robe that had seen better days and carrying a fold-out fan and a paperback hymnbook. To their left sat an out-of-tune, upright piano at which sat a plump, elderly woman who didn't so much as play the piano than assault it. She struck the right keys no more than seventy-five per cent of the time—and that was on the slow hymns. Her key-striking average dropped way, way down on the fast, upbeat ones.

Brother Arnot asked us all to bow our heads while he led us in a "word of prayer." The prayer proved longer than a word. It went on, according to my watch, for ten whole minutes. He followed the prayer with the congregation singing the hymn "Almost Persuaded," which Colonel Loomis himself picked out. I wondered if its title had something to do with his being an auctioneer. I figured it probably did.

Brother Arnot took to the pulpit once we finished the hymn and everybody got comfortable. He slowly opened this huge Bible and turned its golden-edge pages, all the while working his lips. He read from *Mark*: 9:47-48. Brother Arnot pointed out that the words he'd just read weren't just regular words. "No, siree," he said, slapping the

Bible with the back of his hand. "Them's attention-gitting words. They's colored in red, the same color of the blood Christ shed for me and you at Calvary."

He closed the great book, gave it a love pat, and stood in silence for a moment or two, his eyes closed and his lips moving again. As he opened his eyes, Brother Arnot commenced his remarks. "Let me put what I read to you from the *Gospel of Mark* in plain English so there ain't no misunderstanding about it. What it says is this: it's better for a person to enter the kingdom of God with only one eye than be thrown with both eyes into Hell, a place where there's worms what don't never die and a fire what don't never go out.

"You know, I didn't learn about Brother Loomis' death until the lawyer called me about doing the funeral. Amen. Amen. Like most of you, I reckon, I just couldn't believe it. I sure couldn't. Amen.

"After work when I got home, I went to the ice box there in the kitchen and got me out a cold drank. Then, I went out on the back porch and set myself down there on the steps to think about what I was gonna say when it come time for me to preach his funeral. Amen."

He leaned into the pulpit. "I just set there, thinking and thinking. Amen. And about that time, here come the garbage man. Amen. He picked up my garbage can and took it to his truck where he emptied it out. I figured, later on, he'd take all that garbage to the city dump where he'd empty it all into that pit they got there, amen, and them what work out there, they'd set fire to it, amen, so's to burn up as much of it as they could. Amen. And what they couldn't burn, the flies and the worms, they'd have a go at it. Amen.

"I guess iffen you took the time to pick through all that trash and all that garbage and see what people had throwed away, amen, you'd find all kinda stuff, from the cheapest little doodad there is on up to some real expensive thingamajig. Amen."

Brother Arnot paused a few seconds while he took a swallow of water from a Mason jar he had sitting on the side of the pulpit.

"I got to thinking. Amen. You know it's kinda like that when somebody dies what don't know Jesus. Amen." Brother Arnot began to prance about as he preached, going from one side of the platform to the other. "Old Death, he'll come lots of times sneaking up on you—you know, like a pickpocket. And iffen you're a God-fearing, Jesus-believing, Bible-reading Christian, you'll be taken on up to Heaven. Amen. But iffen you ain't, then I'm here to tell you, it's that garbage dump and trash pile they called Hell for you, and I don't care who you are neither. Amen. Yes, sir, I don't care who you are. Amen. Hear what I say?" he yelled as he slapped his Bible.

"No, sir, I don't care one whit who you are, it's Hell for you iffen you don't know Jesus. Unlike the worms out there at the city dump, the worms down there in Hell, *Mark* says they don't never die, no sir. They just gnaw and gnaw. Everybody say amen."

The congregation answered him back with a loud "Amen."

Brother Arnot continued. "And unlike them fires they got out yonder at the city dump, amen, *Mark* says them fires down there in the devil's fields, they just keep on keeping on—just like them ol' worms do. They scorch and burn, morning, noon, and night—don't never go out. And I suspect, the old devil, iffen he'd happen to run outta natural gas, he's got plenty of propane. Why, he's got tanks full of the stuff and knows where he can git more iffen he's a mind to needing more of it. Amen. Yes, sir.

"It don't matter who you are, iffen you don't know Jesus, that's where you're headed. Amen. Down there, everybody's treated just the same. Amen. There ain't no segregation in Hell. Amen. There ain't no middle class, there ain't no high class, there ain't no low class—just the no class. Amen. There ain't no rich. There ain't no poor. Amen. The same kinda worms, amen, and the same kinda fire goes after everybody alike what's sent down there—the white, the black, the red, the yellow, male and female, old and young. Amen and amen."

He paused long enough to take another sip of water. "All this talk about fire, it's kinda making me thirsty," he said as an aside.

Brother Arnot danced around from behind the pulpit. "Yes, sir, when them old worms ain't chawing on you, the fire, it'll be smarting you, barbequing you like you're a pig cut of some sort. You'll be doing like this whenever them tongues of fire starts licking at you." Brother Arnot started hopping around and batting himself, acting like he was on fire, and saying over and over, "Oh! Ouch! Oooh! That hurts! Git me some water, somebody. I'm burning up."

Then he commenced to talking about how persons with certain educations and in certain professions and occupations were going to Hell iffen they didn't accept Jesus as their Lord and Savior. He started with the medical profession but saved the legal profession for last.

Brother Arnot stared straight at me when he decided to pick on the lawyers. "And then," he said, raising a clenched fist and speaking much louder than when he talked about the doctors, the professors, the accountants, and the others, "you might be somebody what's gone to law school, amen, and gotcha self one of them fancy law degrees, amen, and passed the bar exam and hung you out a shingle, amen, and started suing everybody and his brother, gitting rich at the expense of good, decent, hard-working folks, taking their money and, after gitting your cut, giving it to them what don't deserve it—ain't nothing nobody's own fault nowadays, you know. Amen. But even iffen you was a lawyer, and you up and died and you didn't call Jesus your Lord and Savior, you'd burn and be chawed on just like every other sinner in Hell, and maybe even worser. Amen. Them worms down there, I hear tell, just love munching on lawyers. To the demons, they're just like eating strawberry shortcake. Amen and amen."

About that time, the long-necked woman screamed and cried out, "It's gonna rain tonight!"

This caused Brother Arnot to pause, smile down at the woman, and kinda boogie over closer to her. "Say what, sister?"

The woman yelled out again. "Lord, don't let it rain! Please don't!" Then she started jabbering or talking tongue, I couldn't tell which.

Brother Arnot looked down at her, held up an open hand, closed his eyes, and said, "God bless you, sister. God bless you."

Now egged on by the preacher, the woman stood, turned my way, and started shaking an angry finger at me. "And the lawyer—that one sitting right there, y'all—he wouldn't let us have no vault! No, he wouldn't. The mean thing. And poor Colonel Loomis. Look at him, laying there in that old cheap cardboard box the lawyer picked out for him. Tonight, when it rains and the rainwater soaks down into the ground, my uncle's body, it's gonna get all soaking wet. And it'll be the lawyer's fault—the hateful thing.

"Oh, why didn't you let him have a vault? Why didn't you let him have a decent coffin? Why didn't you do it? Why? Why? Why didn't you? I wouldn't treat a dead, mangy dog the way you've treated my dear, sweet uncle, you shyster, you. Oh, the shame of it. And when my sweet, dear uncle finally meets Jesus tonight, he'll be wearing a suit that's soaking wet. This is just plain awful."

By now the whole of the congregation stood on its feet, echoing her complaints and adding insults and accusations of their own, calling me all kinda names. The whole time Brother Arnot just stood there, his arms folded and smiling to beat the band. He also got in a lick of his own, shouting, "And the lawyer wouldn't pay for no limousine for me and Bessie and her brothers to ride in to the church and out to the cemetery and back neither. Don't y'all forget that. Seems to me like he wants all the colonel's money for his own self. And I bet he'll git it too. He's a lawyer, ain't he?" He paused a moment. "Well, ain't he?"

The crowd roared back.

I just sat there taking it. But when this little boy—he couldn't have been more than four-years old—came running up to me and, much to the delight of all those around me, kicked me hard on the shin, I figured it was time for me to get the heck out of there.

As I hurried up the aisle, people continued to yell at me, some even using curse words—right there in church, of all places. Several of them—Hack Hackberry being one of them, hollered out, "Kill all the lawyers." Then somebody else, whose voice also sounded familiar, shouted, "Hey, Deloris, where you headed? Finally gonna get that old pinstripe you're wearing dry-cleaned and pressed?"

Just as I reached the door, somebody let go of a hymnbook, hitting me in my left kidney. Once outside, I jumped into truck and skedaddled.

No telling how many clients I lost that day.

* * * * *

When I got back to town, I gathered up all the things I'd removed from the colonel's house and went through them. I wanted to see if he'd left me any information on where to find the person getting everything he owned, Roda Anne Harrison. He had listed the addresses of Bessie Phillips and her two brothers, Kale and Dale, but had neglected to give one for the Harrison woman.

Now what was I to do? I asked myself.

I called Billy Joe for suggestions. He said I ought to go back out to the colonel's and root around in all the desk drawers and such looking for something that might have it, like an address book or an old envelope of some kind. I asked him if he wanted to go back out there with me.

He told me flat out, "Why hell no, I don't wanna go with you. Do I ever ask you to help me with any of my cases?" Then he hung up.

I guess I spent about thirty minutes or more that afternoon opening drawers to anything that had drawers before I came across an old Christmas card. The postmark on the envelope said it had been mailed four years before from Abilene, Texas. It didn't give a return address, but it was signed, "Love, Roda Anne."

This had to be Roda Anne Harrison, I convinced myself.

I continued the search, but I didn't find anything else.

I knew it wouldn't do me any good to ask the Phillips woman and her brothers if they might know the Harrison woman's address or who she was even. I felt pretty sure they wouldn't help me do anything, after the way they'd acted at his funeral. So, I resigned myself to driving out west in an attempt to find her.

Another thing I knew for absolute certain: this would be one fee I'd earn every cent of, and then some. I wondered how many clients I'd miss out on in the meantime, too.

CHAPTER THREE

I rose early the next morning and drove to the Grease Pit, a one-room greasy spoon set in a cement-block building across from Cooper Junior College. Gasoline and oil signs of all descriptions plastered the whole outside. They also decorated the walls inside, except for the menu board provided by one of the local soft-drink bottlers.

I ate breakfast there at least once a week. It was the only place in town I could get pork brains, cheese grits, scrambled eggs, toast, and coffee, a personal favorite. I sometimes ate supper there, too; like when I had a hankering for a "Lubricator," what they called their hamburger plate. It came with a thick, juicy hamburger that had loads of greasy, fried onion rings and French-fries, and the biggest glass of sweet ice tea in the whole state.

Glory and Rufus Hiers, both in their middle age, ran the place. Glory, a flabby, hard-face woman with unpainted, tight lips, squinting eyes, and short, gray hair, took the orders and ran the cash register (and her mouth) at the bend of a U-shaped counter while Rufus, a man with the face of a happy clown, worked the grill. They never seemed to take any time off. And they were generally friendly, except to each other—well, to be more exact, except Glory to Rufus. From sunup to sundown, she was on his case, cursing him and shaking a balled fist at him for everything and anything. I figured one day, when she wasn't looking, Rufus would have just about enough of her meanness and would let her have it right in the back of her head and later stand trial for assault and, if he hit her hard enough, for murder in the first degree. But so far, he had refrained from attacking her.

I pulled my truck into the parking lot of the Grease Pit a little before sunrise. Lights from inside the restaurant favored the parking spaces closest to the building, distinguishing them from those touched only by the light of dawn. I sat for a moment, watching Glory and Rufus as they made ready for an onslaught of students from the junior college. As yet, none had arrived. They usually came all at once, shortly after seven.

As soon as I walked into the Grease Pit, I got a good whiff of brewing coffee. "Morning, Glory," I said. "That coffee sure does smell good."

Glory smiled back at me. "Course it does, Lawyer Meek. We ain't got no other kind."

I plopped down on one of the round, vinyl stools, wished Rufus a good morning, and ordered my usual, plus an extra helping of cheese grits.

A stack of comic books occupied the stool to my left. They and Glory's constant verbal assaults on her poor husband attracted the students to the diner as much as the Lubricator, their other delicious sandwiches, and their brimstone-hot chili, which the menu dubbed "Antifreeze." Their coffee was so high-test a cup'd been known to keep students awake for an entire week. During exam time, the Grease Pit couldn't serve enough of it.

Glory set a cup of coffee before me and kinda laughed. "Hear they damn near run you outta that auctioneer's funeral yesterday, Deloris. Is that right?"

Her remark surprised me. "You done heard about that already?" I said as I reached for a can of evaporated milk. I wanted it more to dilute the coffee than to alter its flavor.

Glory wiped the top of the counter with the bottom of her apron. "Yeah. Hack Hackberry, he come by here last night. Told us all 'bout it. He was just a'laughing. Said I shoulda seen you. Said he ain't never seen nobody as scared as you were right then. Said you come buckety-buck up the aisle when folks started calling you all kinda names and such. Said he joined in the fun, him and Doc Eleazer did.

Said he yelled out 'Kill all the lawyers,' and Doc, he throwed a hymn book at you. Hit you, too, Hack said. I tell you—"

"That was Doc? He's the one threw it?" It disappointed me Doc would do such a thing, although Hack wasn't above lying about something like that.

Glory waved the air with her hand. "Oh, pshaw. They were just having some fun with you, that's all."

"Some fun," I remarked. "And in a church too."

"Come on now, don't get yourself all outta joint. I don't think he really meant to hit you no how. Probably an accident."

She leaned down, placed her elbows on the counter, and rested her chin in her hands as she brought her eyes up to meet mine. "How'd it start anyway, honey—all that ruckus? Can't say I ever heard of nothing like that happening before. I've heard a time or two of families arguing at funerals over rings and such, but I ain't never heard of nothing like what happened yesterday. You know, folks jumping on the lawyer—not at no funeral, I ain't."

"What about jumping on lawyers, Glory?" Rufus said, walking up, a large bottle of cola in his hand.

Glory stood up straight and whipped around. "Who the hell invited you in on this conversation?" She spun her finger and then pointed toward the grill. "You just turn yourself around and march your skinny butt back to where you belong and get at frying some of that bacon. Them kids, they'll be in here before you know it. Now get cracking. Always gotta know everything, ain't you? Try to make everything your business, doncha?"

Rufus, smiling, dipped his head at me and scurried back to the rear.

"Damn fool, I tell you he's plumb loco. Tell you what he did last night. He woke me up a little after midnight. Said he could swear he'd heard a haint stumbling around in the kitchen. He got up to go see, and when he come back, I said, 'Well, tell me. Did you see it? Did you see a haint?' Know what he said? He said, 'No, but I almost did.' "

She gritted her teeth and made a sucking sound. "Almost seen a haint, my ass. How do you almost see a haint? Never heard anything so stupid in all my born days. He ain't heard nothing. He just dreamed he had."

A moment of pity for Rufus took hold of me, but I let it pass. "You wanna know how it all started there at the funeral?" I asked.

Glory leaned down on the counter again. "Sure would. I asked Hack. But he said he didn't know exactly. Said he had the impression it started down front. Said he was way back there in the rear and didn't quite hear everything what was going on right then. But said he did hear some woman yell out something other, and that might've been the start of it."

I took a sip of my coffee. "That's right. A woman did start it. Some woman named Bessie Phillips."

Glory stood upright again. "Bessie Phillips? Why, I know her. She's got two goofy-looking brothers."

"You know them, you say?"

Glory nodded. "Yeah, sure do. They come in here every so often. They all three work over at the junior college. I think she's a bookkeeper or something in the finance department, and the brothers—I don't rightly know what they do. I think somebody told me one time they both work in student housing or grounds. I dunno."

"I dunno either."

"That woman, she's a hateful thing, she is. Talks to me like I ain't nobody. Wish they wouldn't come in here, but we can't afford to be choosey. And them two brothers of hern, you oughtta hear how she talks to them. Then again, they don't act like they got good sense—not them two don't. When they all come, she always orders for the three of them. And iffen one of brothers wants a piece of pie or something other, she tells them no, they can't have it and then she'll go and order herself a piece for her own self. I ain't never known nobody to be so bossy. Swear to goodness."

I listened to her go on about the three, marveling at how she didn't see the irony there. According to the way she described the Phillips woman, Glory could have been looking at her double.

Glory raised herself up on her tiptoes and looked back where Rufus stood. She watched him for a few seconds, muttering curses to herself.

He had slapped some bacon onto the grill and it had begun to sizzle and give off its captivating, smoky smell. It made my mouth melt, so I told Glory to add a couple of pieces to my order.

She yelled at Rufus, telling him to hurry up with my breakfast and to put a couple of slices of bacon on my plate.

"Does he still want his brains?" Rufus asked, his neck stretched as he looked my way.

I started to answer him, but Glory stamped her foot and beat me to it. "Why, hell yes, he wants them. Did I say he didn't? Where the devil do you come up with these damn stupid questions of yourn? I swear to goodness. Your head is gonna plumb explode from you trying to think, iffen you ain't careful."

She turned back my way, and using a voice far, far different than the one she had just used in speaking to her husband, said, "Whatcha reckon you done, baby? You know, to set that hateful old woman off so?"

"Me? Nothing. I didn't do a blessed thing," I said. "Well, nothing wrong. The only thing I've done is go to a client's funeral and be respectful, doncha know. What I think happened is they got mad—that woman and her brothers—when they learned the colonel—you know, the auctioneer—when they learned he was leaving everything he owned to this woman who lives, near as I can tell, out in Texas.

"I think what they'd planned to do was try and get me to spend as much of the colonel's money as they possibly could rather than let that woman in Texas get her hands on it. They wanted me to buy a vault, which the colonel didn't want, and they wanted me to buy him a real expensive casket. The colonel, he didn't want that either. I believe they got in cahoots with the preacher and the funeral home folks to punish me for not letting them have their way—you know, spend a bunch of his money on stuff he didn't want. I don't think what happened at the funeral could've happened without them allowing it to happen."

"Glory," Rufus called out.

"Hush the hell up," she said without so much as a glance his way. "Doncha see me talking to Deloris, you stupid bastard?"

"Glory," he called again in a timid voice. "Ain't that them what's out yonder?" he said, pointing toward the outside. "I can't see good on account of the window being all fogged up."

"Ain't that who?" she said. "Be specific, dammit. For all I know you could be talking 'bout Lyndon Johnson and that damn fanny-faced vice-president of hisen."

"Them folks you and Deloris been talking 'bout. You know, them Phillipses. They're standing out there, looking at Deloris' truck."

* * * * *

I went outside to where Bessie Phillips and her brothers stood staring at my truck and asked them in a polite voice if I could help them. The two men still wore what appeared to be the same clothes they had on at the funeral—black, out-dated suits with slick trousers, the cuffs of which ended about an inch above their ankle bones. She, on the other hand, was dressed in a simple white blouse, a brown skirt, stockings, and a pair of tan flats with a dohickey of some kind on top. She carried a purse so big it could only have come with a luggage set. The purse hung from her shoulder in such a way it made her body droop to one side, giving her a deformed look.

None of them answered me. They just all three shifted their eyes toward me and chuckled, both men putting a hand to their mouth. So, I asked them again if I could help them.

Bessie shifted her purse from one shoulder to the other and said, "If you were the last lawyer on earth, we wouldn't call on you. Anybody that'd use a milk truck for a law office has to be a little off, if you know what I mean." She twirled a finger at her temple.

Both brothers snorted their agreement and sniggered, sissy-like through their noses. They sounded like piglets enjoying a tit.

"Then whatcha want?" I asked.

One of the brothers opened his mouth like he was about to say something when Bessie motioned to him to keep quiet.

"We were just looking at your truck. That's all. I'd love to have a picture of it. I bet it's the only one like it in the whole wide world. Somebody oughtta send it in to Ripley's 'Believe it or Not.' " She paused and glanced at her brothers. "And your name, is it really Deloris? If I'm not mistaken, that's a girl name, isn't it?"

They all three laughed.

"Well, y'all just keep away from my truck," I said, my voice tinged with a hint of anger. "And another thing. About my name. It's 'Deloris' with an 'I.' Not an 'E'."

I wheeled around to go back inside and eat my breakfast.

"Actually, Lawyer Meek," Bessie said, "we're delighted to have run into you."

I turned back around.

"Say what?"

"We just wanted to let you know that we've got an appointment with a lawyer this morning. We're gonna see about suing you and Colonel Loomis' estate. How's that grab you, huh? You the one getting sued for a change."

Bessie and her brothers smiled at each other.

Even though the Phillipses had hinted at taking some sort of legal action against the estate and me the day before, what Bessie said still surprised me a little. "Really?" I said. Then it was my turn to laugh. "Go on ahead and do it. All y'all'll be doing is wasting your money. Heck, y'all won't even get to first base."

"Oh, is that right?" Bessie said. "Well, nobody's asking you, Mr. Meek. No, I think we'll just get our advice from a real lawyer—Meriwether Suffridge, IV, Esquire. I understand the two of you know each other."

I knew him. I had gone up against Suffridge once before in a probate court proceeding, and I'd got my tail handed to me on a platter.

* * * * *

I delayed leaving town until I could talk to Billy Joe Pratt. I telephoned him from Mr. Kingry's office and told him I was about to head for Texas and I needed to talk to him about something before I left.

"You're leaving for Texas today, you say?" Billy Joe asked.

"Well, I'd plan to. I wanna go and try to find that woman soon as I can, doncha know."

"How you going?"

"Driving. Taking the truck."

"Your truck?" Billy Joe said with a laugh. "You sure that thing'll make it? Excuse me a second, Deloris."

The muted voice of Dixie St. John traveled over the line, but I couldn't understand what she'd said.

Billy Joe came back on the phone. "Dixie wants to know whether you're going through Baggett?"

"I think so. Yeah."

Billy Joe repeated my answer, and then he said, "You mentioned you needed to talk to me about something."

I told Billy Joe about what Bessie Phillips had said to me.

His response didn't sit too well with me. He showed me no sympathy whatsoever.

"So," he said, "they wanna sue you in an effort to get the will set aside, do they? Well, if Suffridge agrees to take their case, he's the best lawyer in town to do it, all right."

"But Billy Joe, they don't have no suit," I said.

"So what if they don't?" he said.

"Whatcha mean?"

"Why heck, man, Suffridge's got just as much right to make money off the colonel's death as you do." Billy Joe laughed. "You're familiar with the Lawyer's Prayer, aren't you?"

"Lawyer's Prayer? No, I don't think I am."

"It goes, *God bless those who sue my clients.* I expect Suffridge will repeat that prayer before the sun goes down."

"Well, if he does bring suit, would you consider doing me a favor?" I said. "That's the main reason I'm calling you."

"What kind of favor?" Billy Joe's voice sounded kinda guarded.

I was about to ask him to represent the colonel's estate and me as executor when his secretary said something to him. I couldn't make out what she said, but then Billy Joe said, "Like hell you are." After she said something else, only louder, he said, using a quieter tone, "I'll talk to you about it in a minute. Okay? Can't you see I'm on the phone with Deloris?" The next words spoken came from Dixie. They sounded like she said, "If you won't let me off, then I quit."

After a long pause during which only soft mumbling reached my ear—I got the impression Billy Joe had his hand held over the phone—he came back on the line and said, "Dixie just told me she's going on paid vacation. She wants to know if she can ride with you as far as Baggett, that is, if you can wait till in the morning to leave."

I couldn't believe my ears. "You say Dixie wants a ride with me? Wants me to take her to Baggett?" I could hardly talk I was so excited about the prospect of having Dixie St. John spend a little time with me. I'd long had a crush on her, as did Billy Joe, but he'd never admit it. "Why, heck yeah, I can wait. One day won't make no difference. Tell her I'll pick her up at your office at nine in the morning. Okay?"

Billy Joe told her what I'd said, and she said something back to him; but I couldn't tell what it was.

"Deloris?"

"Yeah?"

"She said make it nine-thirty."

"Okay," I said. "And Billy Joe?"

"Yeah?"

"How come she wants to go to Baggett?"

"I'll ask her."

Billy Joe must've put his hand over the mouthpiece again because I didn't hear anything for a moment or two.

"Deloris?" he said, coming back on the phone.

"Yeah?"

"She said it wasn't any of your, to use her words, *damn business* why she wants to go, and if you insisted on knowing why then she's not gonna ride with you. Said she'll find another way."

"Billy Joe, just tell her I'll see her at nine-thirty in the morning."

I didn't care if Dixie didn't want to tell me why she wanted to go to Baggett. Her reason for wanting a ride didn't really matter all that much to me. I was just curious, that's all.

As thrilled as I, a single, never-been-married, pushing-thirty bachelor, was at spending at least two hours or more with one of the most beautiful creatures in the world while taking her someplace, I still had the threat of a lawsuit by Bessie Phillips and her brothers hanging over me at a time when I needed to leave town. I again broached the subject of Billy Joe's doing me a favor.

He didn't sound very happy about my wanting one. "Deloris," he said, "every time you ask me to do something for you I wind up spending time away from my own law practice or spending money. Another thing, you never, ever listen to me or do what I tell you to."

"It won't be like that this time, though. I promise."

"And why not?"

"Because what I want you to do is represent me and Colonel Loomis' estate if Suffridge does bring suit against us for them. I'll pay you your usual rate. I'd handle it myself except I feel like I oughtta go find this woman soon as I can, doncha know. I can't be putting off trying to do that while sitting around waiting on a lawsuit that might or might not be brought."

Billy Joe didn't say anything for a while. The only sound that came from the other end of the phone was his breathing and what sounded like a match striking. I figured, as he smoked, he was weighing the pros and cons of agreeing to represent the colonel's estate and me. Finally, he came back on the phone, telling me he'd agree to take the case if one was brought, and he'd call Suffridge and tell him about it so there wouldn't be any mix-up about the service of process and so forth, being I'd be gone for a spell.

"And, Deloris," he said, speaking almost in a whisper, "one more thing. Don't make the mistake of trying to make out with Dixie while she's with you. She'd claw your eyes out. I'd hate see you walking around with a cane."

Knowing him like I did, Billy Joe wasn't giving me the warning for my own protection. He was looking out for his own interest.

CHAPTER FOUR

I was so excited about Dixie St. John's desire to accompany me as far as Baggett I didn't sleep two hours the whole night long. When I realized sleep was a lost cause, I got up, showered, shaved, dressed, and loaded my clothes and things into the office area of my truck. I considered going out to eat breakfast, but then I realized the Grease Pit wouldn't open for a couple of hours. So, I just made me some toast and a cup of Sanka.

I turned on the TV, but the only thing I could pick up with my rabbit ears was a test pattern. That being the case, I turned the TV off, parked myself into my reclining chair, and picked up a book I'd started about a week before but had put aside after reading only the first eight pages. The next thing I knew the telephone was ringing off the hook. I jumped up to go answer it. When I looked at my watch I couldn't believe the time. Nine-thirty-five! It didn't take me but one second to figure out who was calling. It just had to be Dixie.

And Dixie it was, calling me from, she said, a phone booth.

Speaking fast so as not to give her a chance to get a word in edgewise, I apologized, making up some lie about not being able to get my truck started. I told Dixie I must've flooded it whenever I went to crank it up and I had to wait till the gas cleared out of the carburetor before I could try starting it again. I told her the reason I didn't call was I didn't know how I might get in touch with her because I knew Billy Joe wasn't ever at work on time and I assumed she'd be waiting for me outside.

I don't think she believed a word of it. She said if I wasn't there in ten minutes, she'd find another way.

I made it to Billy Joe's office in seven minutes, running two red lights and one stop sign getting there. Dixie stood at the curb by a large suitcase, her arms folded and one foot tapping a hundred miles an hour. Although she had one of the most beautiful faces God ever made, that didn't keep her from looking mean as the devil whenever something didn't go to please her. I swear she could get riled up the fastest of any woman I had ever seen or heard of even. I think she had convinced herself that her good looks entitled her to be that way or any other way she wanted. Billy Joe once said to me, "Deloris, if just one time when Dixie was a little girl some little boy had whipped her ass real good she'd been a different person today." I agreed with him one hundred percent.

I pulled my refashioned Divco up next to where she stood with an armload of what turned out to be romance magazines. I wished her a good morning and gave her a big smile

Her first words to me? "If you knew how embarrassing this is for me to have to ride in this awful-looking thing, you would've rented a car. You know that? A durn milk truck. A purple-painted one at that."

I hopped down from the truck and hurried around to grab her suitcase. It was all I could do to carry it to the back of the truck, as heavy as it was. How she got it to where she'd been standing I hadn't a clue. The whole time I struggled with the durn thing I kept thinking one word—hernia. I said to her, "Whatcha got in here, Dixie? Bricks?"

"Yeah," she said, smart-mouth like. "What of it? I'm building a house. Two stories."

I slid the suitcase into the back, pushed my spine back in place with the heel of my hand, and went around and opened the passenger-side door for her. I think she would've stood there all day if I hadn't opened it. Dixie believed strongly in women's rights, one of the most important ones being—for her, anyway—men, whether they're gentlemen or not and no matter their age or physical condition, open doors for women whether they are ladies or not or wanted men to open the doors or not.

She climbed into the truck and laid her magazines on the floor between the two seats in the cab. Once she took her seat, she began twisting around on it so that for a second or two I feared she might screw herself slap into the thing. When I came around on the other side, I found her peering into the passenger-side outside mirror. She pushed back at her hair a couple of times and turned one end of a tube of lipstick as she made an "O" with her mouth. Then she went about applying the stuff to her lips as though she were engaged in some kind of sacred ritual.

"Can I open the door now?" I asked as kindly as I knew how. "I don't wanna cause you to mess up nothing, doncha know."

She leaned back and dropped her lipstick into her purse. "Yeah. Let's go. You've wasted enough time as it is."

"I didn't realize you were in such a hurry," I said as I settled in behind the wheel.

Dixie pointed straight ahead. "Drive."

I drove.

* * * * *

I guess we must've gone about two or three miles before I attempted to engage Dixie in any real conversation. When I remarked on the nice weather we had to travel in, all she'd say was "Drive." After that happened three times, I just shut up and did like she told me to do and kept my thoughts to myself.

When we came up on this filling station about thirty miles from town, she said, "Pull in there. I need to use the ladies' room."

That was to be the first of many stops like that. I think her bladder must've been about the size of a walnut.

Anyway, when she got back into the truck her attitude had swung one-hundred and eighty degrees. Why, sugar wouldn't melt in her mouth, and she just talked and talked, mainly about Billy Joe and how unappreciative he was of her and how lazy he was. "That's one reason I wanted to get out of the office for a little while," she declared. "To show him how much he depends on me." She laughed. "I wonder what he's gonna do now when people telephone and he doesn't have me to answer it and tell them, *He's in conference.* Conference, my foot. He wouldn't know what a conference is. If anything, he'd think it had something to do with football."

She leaned back in her seat as if in thought and laughed again. "Know what I think? I think the number one qualification to be a legal secretary is to be good at lying. At least for Billy Joe, it is."

"Well," I said, "are you good at it?"

"The best," she said with a nod. "In fact, the very best."

We rode on for a mile or two without either of us saying anything. I'd turn to look at her every now and then, and she'd smile at me like I was her preacher or sugar daddy or somebody. I wanted to ask her in the worst sort of way why she wanted to ride with me as far as Baggett, but I decided to let sleeping dogs lie. I wasn't about to say something that'd get her aggravated with me. I still had a long way to go before I dropped her off, and I didn't want to be miserable. For the most part, I kept my hands on the steering wheel, my mouth closed, my ears opened, and, except when I'd sneak a peep at my traveling companion, my eyes on the road.

After a while, she started up again and asked me what I knew about the woman I needed to find. I told her I didn't know a thing about her other than Colonel Loomis left everything he owned to her and indications were, judging from the envelope of the Christmas card she'd sent him from Abilene four years ago, she might live way out in Texas.

She harrumphed. "That's it? That's all you know about the woman? Why, that's the stupidest thing I ever heard. And you're a lawyer? No wonder those people wanna sue you. I would too, if I were them. Your man sounds crazy as a loon to me, leaving all his money and property to somebody without even telling you how to get in touch with her. I bet you don't even know his connection with her, do you?"

Without giving me a chance to answer, Dixie continued with her questions.

"Well, do you know? Is she kin to him somehow? An ex-girlfriend? Who is she?"

I slowed down for a pickup truck ahead of me that had braked and signaled a left turn. "I dunno. I've told you all I know about her."

"What I don't understand is why you didn't do more to find out her address when you took him the will. Seems to me, a first-year law student would've known to do that."

Dixie was starting to get under my skin. "I told him I'd need it. He acted like he understood I would. How was I to know he wouldn't leave it somewhere I could find it?"

"Well anyway, she might be dead, for all you know, or she might've mailed that card from Abilene as she was passing through."

"That's true," I said.

Dixie continued on. "If you want my opinion, you won't never, ever find that woman. Wanna bet me? Yes, sir, you should've made sure you had her address before you even left his house that day. You and Billy Joe, you both take the cake. You know that? And you each one call yourself a lawyer. Tell you what you need to do. You need to turn around and go back."

I laughed. "And if I did that, how would you get to Baggett?"

She didn't answer me.

I drove about twenty more miles with her laying in again on Billy Joe and all his faults and on her former employer and all his. She bragged about how she had Billy Joe completely under her thumb. I told her I knew that already. That seemed to please her because as soon as I said it she crossed her arms, looked straight ahead, and got this big grin on her face.

And then wouldn't you know it? She needed to go to the restroom again.

As it was, I needed a break, too, plus some gasoline. I pulled into this combination country store and filling station and parked beneath an overhang between the gas pumps and several stacks of crates filled with empty soft-drink bottles. Dixie, in as big a hurry as I have ever seen anybody, jumped from the truck before it came to a complete stop. Dodging oil puddles on the ground, she scampered up the steps, past a screen door, and into the store.

I wondered what kind of restroom she would find inside, if she found one at all. The building needed a paint job, except for its south side and its roof. A big soft-drink sign covered the former while the latter advertised a roadside attraction in Tennessee. Metal signs promoting everything from liver pills to cigarettes to fertilizer plastered much of the front. The double screen doors out front, both full of holes, advertised a bread brand in broken, faded letters.

I remained in the truck, waiting for someone to come pump my gas. I blew the horn, but no one came. After I waited a few more minutes, I decided to fill the gas tank myself. As I stood there watching the gallons of Ethyl add up, a man in a late model automobile pulled in behind my truck. The driver sat there staring at my truck for a minute or two and then headed my way, walking like a man in a hurry.

"Sir! Sir! Could I please have a word with you," he hollered.

The man, short and slim and sorta "frenchy" looking, wore a double-breasted blue suit with a red rose in its lapel, a white shirt, red tie, and snappy black shoes. His hair, which was black as tar and parted in the middle, was all combed back and slick looking, and he'd grown a thin little mustache over a pair of some really thick lips and beneath this long, sharp nose. His eyes were as gray as gun metal. My initial impression of the man was of a person whose promissory note I wouldn't co-sign, even at gunpoint.

"Good morning," he said, his hand outstretched. He angled his head at my truck. "You really a lawyer, like it says there?"

I wiped my hand on my trouser leg and took hold of his, but only for a second or two. "Reckon so. I still get notices to pay bar dues."

"Name's Napier. Charles Thomas Napier. Mr. Meek is it?"

"You can call me Deloris."

"Deloris? But ain't that a name you give a girl?"

"No, it's a boy name. And since I got something I can grab hold of, I guess that makes me a boy."

Napier acted like he didn't know whether to laugh or not. He just put his hands into his pants pockets and kicked at the ground, giving me the impression he was in no mood for joking around.

He nodded toward the store. "I think you might could be of some help to me. The man who runs this place, he's the magistrate hereabouts—you know, a judge. He's got his courtroom there in the back. I got to go in front of him in about twenty minutes."

"What for?"

"They say I indecently exposed myself."

"Did you?"

"Hell, no. Of course I didn't."

"Uh-huh."

"Reckon you'd be interested in representing me?"

"Depends."

"On what?"

"You pay me before the trial starts."

Napier's eyes widened. "Pay you up front, you mean? How much?"

"You got two hundred on you?"

"Two hundred? How much afterward?"

"Two hundred total. Win or lose. Appeal, though, it'd be extra."

Napier gritted his teeth. "Gosh, I was hoping to use what money I had to go toward a fine."

"You can still do that, if that's what he sentences you to instead of having them haul you off to the chain gang."

He stood there not saying anything for a few moments.

While I waited for him to think over my proposal, I finished with the refueling and hooked the nozzle back onto the pump.

"How about I give you a check, Mr. Meek?"

I shook my head. "Two hundred dollars cash money. I don't mean you any disrespect, but I've been gypped before by clients who paid with a check. I finally learned my lesson, though. Money up front. No checks. Checks are for merchants and such. Not for lawyers, especially lawyers representing criminal defendants. They're kinda high-risk, doncha know."

"I ain't no criminal. I sell used cars for 'Dodd's Dollar Down Auto.' "

"You ain't no criminal yet, you mean."

All of a sudden, his eyes stuck out like they were on stems. "Jesus!" he exclaimed. "Would you look at what just came around the corner?"

I glanced over his shoulder and watched Dixie as she stomped toward us, her heels kicking up dirt. She looked fit to be tied.

She flounced up to me, not once appearing to notice Napier, who couldn't take his eyes off her. "Why'd you stop here, Deloris?" she roared. "Do you know the only place I could go was a durn old privy out back of the store. A privy! You hear me? A privy. Filthy durn place. Had spiders and I don't know what all. And it had a smell like you couldn't believe. Another thing, all they had for paper was a used geometry book with all these real slick pages for you to tear out. Can you believe a geometry—?"

It was then she noticed Napier for the first time.

She tilted her head to the side. "And just who's this guy? Friend of yours?"

Napier introduced himself, grinning at her and offering her his hand. She refused it, giving him a haughty look.

Once she had calmed down enough that I could talk to her, I told her about Napier's trouble and what he wanted of me.

"You gonna do it?" she asked, stepping back and giving Napier a sizing up.

Napier went for his wallet and withdrew a wad of bills. "Here, Mr. Meek. Here's the two hundred you want."

I didn't reach for it. "But you haven't told me anything about what happened. I may not want your money. I might not be able to do you any good. Besides, we've—"

Dixie interrupted. "Let him talk, why don't you?"

I closed my eyes for a couple of seconds and took a deep breath. It took all I could do to stifle the urge to hit back at Dixie somehow for scolding me in front of a would-be client. I'd seen her do that to Billy Joe before, but he always just laughed it off. So, I chose to follow his example.

"Okay," I said, laughing, "tell us whatcha know."

"It's kinda embarrassing." Napier dipped his head toward Dixie. "Can she step over yonder by those drink crates while me and you talk?"

Before I could answer, Dixie spoke for the two of us—not that I intended for her to do it. "No, I can't. Now," she said, gesturing, "out with it."

I started to protest Dixie's putting her nose into my business again, but then I thought what the hell.

Napier told us a little bit about the prosecuting witness and related what she claimed had happened. He maintained it was a total lie, saying the woman, who lived across the street from him, had a crush on him. He said he had refused several times to date her, and she had cursed him after his last refusal. He went on to say he believed the woman swore out the warrant to get back at him.

His story made sense to me, but I'd practiced law long enough to know that criminal defendants always put a good spin on things, even after they're convicted. If you visited the state pen and talked to some convicts, you'd be surprised how few of them would own on up to what they did.

Right as he finished talking, an old, late-model car with rusted doors, a cracked windshield, and a dented left-front fender pulled into the parking lot and parked close to the soft drink sign. Two women, dressed in long, flowered skirts and white blouses and carrying tiny red purses, exited the car and headed for the front door steps. One, the older and far slimmer of the two, stood at least a foot and a half taller than the other. When side-by-side, they appeared to spell the word "lo."

As I could've guessed, one of the women, the short, round one, turned out to be Napier's accuser. The poor girl gave a new meaning to the saying, "she has a face only a mother could love."

When they walked past the three of us, the younger woman stuck her tongue out at Napier as if to say, "I'll learn you a thing or two." For his part, Napier kept his cool and ignored the greeting.

Dixie watched the women until they disappeared into the store. She turned to Napier and me. "I've got an idea that I guarantee will keep your new client outta jail, but I want half the fee to tell y'all what it is."

I couldn't believe I'd heard her right. "What'd you just say, Dixie? You want half my fee? I can't do that. That'd be unethical. I can't split a legal fee with a lay—"

"Look on it as a fee paid to an expert, and I'm the expert—best one you'll ever have. I promise you I can save your buddy there, but like I said it'll cost you half the fee for me to tell you how to do it." Dixie spoke with the conviction of a West Virginia snake handler at a Sunday morning worship service featuring brand new snakes.

"And just what if it doesn't work?" I said.

Dixie threw up her hands. "Then he goes to jail, and you don't owe me anything. Simple as that."

"Hey," Napier said, "that doesn't sound right to me. Deloris could deliberately lose the case and keep the two hundred bucks. I don't like that deal."

"How about if you're found guilty he refunds your fee?" she said.

"I'm not going along with that," I said.

"Then I won't tell you my idea," she said.

My curiosity got the best of me. After mulling it over some, I agreed to Dixie's terms, proving that curiosity could do more than kill a cat. In my case, it wiped out at least half of a fee I would get for agreeing to represent an accused criminal, if not the whole thing should he be found guilty. But after hearing Dixie explain her idea, I had to admit she had come up with a clever defense. It had all the earmarks of a winner. When Napier handed me his two hundred dollars, I gave Dixie half of it, so confident was I of success.

*****

The magistrate, the Honorable Cleveland Sconyers, made us wait for thirty minutes or more before he told us he was ready to start. He had several store customers who required his attention, and their purchases apparently meant more to him than the administration of justice.

While we waited for the magistrate to complete his business transactions, I tossed Dixie an extra key to my truck and asked her to fetch a law book from my "library."

"Which one?" she asked.

"Doesn't matter. Just the biggest one on the shelf."

"You don't care which?"

"Nope."

Dixie looked at me like I was crazy and hurried off.

She made it back in less than three minutes. She brought me a thick, red-covered book entitled *Simpson on Contracts*.

"Will this one do?" she said, handing me the book.

I nodded. "Perfect."

She stood staring at me, bending her fingers back and forth into her palm. I took it to mean she wanted an explanation about the law book.

"Just for your information," I said, talking low as I held up the book, "this is just a prop. Greatest fear a country magistrate has is a lawyer who comes to court carrying a law book."

Dixie made a face. "Yeah. Right."

I went on inside the "courtroom" and sat down at one of three tables the magistrate had arranged in a T-formation with his table at the bottom of the "T." The prosecuting witness and her mother sat behind the table to my right. A goofy looking deputy sheriff, who had just arrived with his siren blaring, stood between us, making funny noises with his lips that sounded like a motor running.

The so-called "courtroom" was nothing but a small, hot storage space stacked with cases of soft drinks, boxes of canned goods, sacks of fertilizers and seeds, and piles of dry goods. A large, loud window fan drew air in through an open door and two open windows. Every now and then a chicken with its head bobbing would strut up to the doorway, peek in, and beat a fast retreat. I could only assume one or more of us looked threatening. I figured it had to be the prosecuting witness the chicken feared. She sat, staring wild-eyed straight ahead, her face taut, sweat pouring down her puffy cheeks as her ample chest heaved up and down with each breath she took. Her mother made a few efforts to engage her in conversation, but the daughter would have none of it, paying her no mind at all.

Dixie and Napier didn't wait inside the courtroom with the rest of us. As part of Dixie's plan, they remained within the store proper. I busied myself putting some items I had in a small cardboard box I'd found on the floor inside the store. I planned to try something Billy Joe told me he understood a lawyer from Atlanta once pulled on an eyewitness.

Finished with his business, Judge Sconyers sauntered into the courtroom, sipping a Dr. Pepper. He offered to get each of us one if we wanted it. Only the deputy sheriff took him up on the offer. I laughed when that happened because I remembered what Billy Joe told me one time. "Deloris," he said, "there ain't never been a policeman who ever refused to take something that's been offered to him free of charge." The magistrate told the deputy to go get himself one, and away he flew.

While we waited on the deputy to return, Judge Sconyers sat down behind his table and looked around. When his eyes fell on me, he said, "You the defendant, bub?"

"No, sir," I said. "The lawyer."

He snorted. "Coulda fooled me. You got proof you a lawyer?"

I passed him my business card. That and my say-so was the only proof I had beyond my truck outside and the testimony I could offer from myself and from Dixie.

The magistrate read the card and looked up at me. "So, according to this here, you represent the *catching hell*. That right?"

I stood. "All the time."

He inserted the card into his shirt pocket. "Well, then, where's the one who's about to catch it today?"

"Just a minute, Your Honor, and I'll get him for you. He was out there in your store last I saw him. Him and the lady with him, they were picking through the magazine rack."

I went to the door and motioned for Dixie and Napier to join us in the courtroom. They waited until I got back to my chair before they came through the door. When they made their entrance, they were holding hands and making goo-goo eyes at each other. When Napier reached his chair, he turned his cheek toward Dixie and she kissed it—an action that turned my stomach. Dixie then sat down on some boxes of canned goods a yard or so behind Napier. Meanwhile, the magistrate sat drop-mouth, never taking his eyes off Dixie.

After she crossed her long, shapely legs, the magistrate blew out some breath and asked the deputy and me if we were prepared to move forward with a bench trial, meaning a trial before a judge alone, sitting without a jury. We both said yes.

The deputy called Vera Dell Blocker, the o-shaped younger woman, to step forward. The magistrate swore her in as a witness and then ordered me not to object to any question that might be leading. "I wanna speed things up. I don't want no lawyer shenanigans getting this thing all long and drawn out. I've got customers that might need attending to," he said. "The law-abiding, paying kind, not some no-count hoping for a get-out-of-jail-free card"—he pointed to Napier—" like him right there. Understand me, Counselor?"

"Yes, sir," I said. "I'm in a bit of a hurry my own self."

The deputy, a serious, slow talking man in his late thirties or early forties, got right to the point in his examination of Vera Dell. "You know the defendant? That man yonder? Fella with the mustache. The one dressed in—"

The magistrate slapped the table. "For crying out loud, Deputy, she knows who you're talking about. Get on with it," he growled.

The top of the deputy's bald head glowed a bright red. He took a sip of his Dr. Pepper. "Yes, sir. I wasn't sure she understood who I was asking her about. I wanted to—"

"Just finish your drink and hush," the magistrate said, interrupting. "And take a seat over yonder. I'll do the questioning. I declare to goodness." He turned to the witness who sat to his right. "Ma'am, you know that man yonder, don't you?" he said, indicating.

Vera Dell, who had been bent over scratching her ankle, sat up straight. "The deputy man?"

The magistrate shook his head. "No, ma'am. That man sitting over there."

"That big fella? Ain't never seen him before a while ago."

The magistrate dropped his head and exhaled audibly. "Not him. The other one." The magistrate put a hand to his ear. "Hold on a second. Was that somebody come in the store? I thought I heard somebody."

We all looked at each other. Nobody said anything.

"Well?" the magistrate said.

"No, sir. I don't see nobody."

"I ain't asking you about that. I'm asking you if you know that other fella. That one there? The little one." The magistrate pointed at Napier. "You seen him before?"

"Oh, him? Yes, sir. Quite a few times."

"Where abouts?" the magistrate asked.

"Across the street in that duplex. It's got a little porch there."

"Did something happen when you saw him"—he picked up the arrest warrant and glanced at it—"when you saw him on August 8, 1965?"

"He come out that afternoon late, out onto that little porch. Had his subpoena in his hand."

"You saw this?"

"Did I see it? Scared me half to death. Still does when I think about it," she said as she fanned herself with an open hand.

The magistrate turned to the deputy. "That all, Deputy?"

The deputy stood. "I reckon so. I ain't really talk to her much about it. I don't—"

The magistrate scratched his head. "All right, sir. Tell me your name again, Counselor. I disremember it."

I stood. " 'Meek,' Your Honor. 'Deloris Meek.' "

"Yeah, that's it. 'Deloris Meek'? Your first name's 'Deloris'? Whatcha doing with a girl's name?"

"It's 'Deloris' with an 'I,' Your Honor."

"That's supposed to make some kinda difference?"

I hunched my shoulders. "To me it does. Yes, sir."

"I see," he said with a nod and leaned back. "All right, sir. Proceed, but if you hear somebody come in the store, you stop and tell me. Okay?"

I walked up to the witness, carrying the box I'd found and into which I had placed a comb, a jackknife, two matchbooks, a dime, and five-dollar bill.

"Miss Blocker," I began, "how quickly did this thing happen?"

"He come out. I seen that awful thing he had, holding it. He run back inside. Just like that."

"Say about five seconds? You know, one . . . two . . . three . . . four . . . five. About like that?"

"You could say that—only it might've been quicker."

"Weren't you mad at him because he wouldn't take you out on a date? Take you to the picture show or dancing someplace?"

"No. He tell you that? He's a big old story-teller. I wouldn't go out with him if he was the last man on earth."

"So, he showed you what now?"

"I done told you."

"Tell us again. I wanna make sure I heard you right."

"His subpoena. He showed me his subpoena."

"You sure now that's what it was?"

"I sure am. Yes."

"A subpoena. All right then, what color was it?"

"Kinda pinkish, purplish."

"A pinkish, purplish subpoena?" I took a step or two backward. "Had you ever seen a subpoena before?"

"First time. I'd heard tell about them, though. Some old nasty talking girls I work with at the dime store told me about them and what they were for and all. Made me sick."

"Could you tell if the subpoena had any writing on it?"

"Writing on it? You wanna know if his subpoena had writing on it?" She scratched the back of her neck and shook her head. "I guess it coulda had some on it, but it'd been so little bitty I couldna read it from where I was standing at." Vera Dell looked puzzled. "Could I ask you something? Why would it have writing on it? Are they all thataway?"

I nodded. "Why, yeah. Every subpoena I've ever seen had writing on it."

She sat, looking to the side toward the floor with her mouth open and her brow wrinkled as though deep in thought.

I pressed on. "But you are telling me and the judge here that you're absolutely certain it was a subpoena," I said, staring straight at the magistrate.

She looked up, folded her arms, and raised her nose at me. "I most certainly am."

"And what was he doing with it, this subpoena, this pinkish, purplish thing, as you describe it?"

"What was he doing with it?" She paused a second or two. "Just standing there, holding it."

"How far away is his porch from your place?"

"Across the street some twenty or thirty yards, I reckon. I really dunno exactly. Not far. I ain't measured it none. Didn't know I was supposed to." She turned to the magistrate. "Was I supposed to, Your Honor? Ain't nobody told me to."

The magistrate did not respond other than sigh and motion for me to continue. He looked kinda tired and worn out when he did it.

I eased up close to Vera Dell. "I'm gonna hand you a box and ask you to look inside it for no more than five seconds, which I'm gonna count out loud for you. Okay?"

"Okay, but it sounds kinda stupid to me."

"Now don't look until I tell you to." I handed her the box. "Okay, look. One . . . two . . . three . . . four . . . five. Stop looking."

The witness looked up.

"What did you see?"

"What'd I see? A comb, a matchbook that said, 'Baby's Supper Club,' another one that has an ad for a correspondence course in welding, and a five-dollar bill. Oh yeah, a Mercury dime dated 1937. You had a knife in there too. It's chipped on the side. I can tell you the serial number on the five-dollar bill, if you want me to. You want me to?"

I shook my head, thoroughly unnerved by her response. Vera Dell's answer had not only rattled me, it had embarrassed me, too. My face aflame, I turned around and looked at Dixie. She just rolled her eyes at me. I tried to act like Vera Dell's response didn't bother me any, although I knew the color of my face gave me away. I hastened to ask her another question to show she had not intimidated me. "Did you see anything else?"

"In the box, you mean? Nothing but the bottom of it." She put a finger to her lips and looked away for a moment. "Come to think of it, I did. I also saw something that looked like mouse droppings and a dead roach—a little one. Look and see if you don't see them in there, too. Filthy things."

The magistrate cocked his head to the side. "Any more lawyer tricks, Counselor?"

I returned to my chair. "That's all I have, Your Honor. I mean—"

The magistrate sat back and folded his arms. "Any more questions you want me to ask, Deputy?"

The deputy stood. "No, sir. I think that about wraps it up. But could I ask you something else?"

The magistrate responded with a nod.

"Can I get me another Dr. Pepper when we're finished up here, Your Honor?"

"I guess so. But just one. If you leave with it, bring me back the bottle. They cost me two cents deposit." He glanced my way. "All right, sir. Your turn."

I stood. "No testimony, Your Honor. Defense rests. But I do have a motion to make."

Judge Sconyers pulled a pen from his shirt pocket and shifted a legal pad from one corner of his table to its center. "All right, sir. Be glad to hear from you. Make it quick."

"Your Honor, the defense moves for a directed verdict of not guilty. The prosecution has not proved any crime occurred. The witness made it quite clear the defendant, Mr. Napier, had only a subpoena in his hand. I know of no law in this state that declares the holding of a subpoena amounts to indecent exposure."

The magistrate smiled. "Mr. Meek, sir, you know as well as I do the lady—what's the word?—misspoke. We all know what she meant."

I paused just long enough to pick up the law book on contracts. I opened it and turned a few pages. I pretended to read from it to myself. "Yes, here's what I'm looking for, Your Honor," I said, slapping the right-side page with my free hand. "There's authority here—"

"Now whatcha reading from, Counselor?" Judge Sconyers asked, pen poised to write though his voice hinted of skepticism.

"Oh, this? It's a law book, Your Honor."

"Gimme that. I wanna see it."

He had me. I didn't know what to do. I hadn't counted on the magistrate's wanting a close-up look at the book. I had overplayed my hand. The law of contracts had nothing to do with the crime of indecent exposure. If he was smart enough to run a store, then I recognized too late he'd know that too. "Your Honor, this book . . . now, what I'm looking at . . . it doesn't exactly . . ."

Before I could finish my sentence, Dixie stood and addressed the magistrate. "Judge, can I say something?"

Judge Sconyers first looked at Dixie with a surprised look on his face. Then he smiled. "Why, of course, young lady." He gestured for her to step from behind Napier. "What would you like to tell me? Take all the time you need."

Dixie smiled at the magistrate, her head turned slightly down and to the right. "Your Honor, sir, am I so ugly that poor Charlie here," she turned and ran her long, fingers through Napier's greasy hair, "would prepare to trade for another woman by baiting her with, as she calls it, his 'subpoena'? Am I, Your Honor?"

Judge Sconyers looked at Vera Dell, grimaced, and then looked at Dixie. He leaned far back in his chair and sat there staring at her for I don't know how long, all the while with his arms resting in his lap and his tongue set against his top lip. Done with that, he straightened himself up. "I'm ready to rule. Now tell me, ma'am, what name you go by? I don't think you said."

Dixie fluttered her eyes. "Dixie. Dixie St. John, Judge, Your Honor . . . Sir." After the word "sir," Dixie slowly licked her lips, beginning with the top one.

"Yeah. Okay. I tell you what. You're right. He wouldn't do that. Not unless he'd gone plumb loco, he wouldn't. Been my experience folks don't usually trade down. Case dismissed."

And with that, his Honor rose from his chair and left the room, singing the first line of the refrain to "Dixie."

* * * * *

As we prepared to leave, I watched Dixie from inside my truck as she strolled over to Napier's car to tell him goodbye. He sat behind the steering wheel with his window open and his motor running. I saw her lean into the window and look down. Then, all of a sudden, she stepped backwards and began to laugh, a hand to her chest. That's when I heard her say, "Is that what all the fuss was about?"

A moment or so, Dixie opened the door and slid onto the seat beside me, still laughing.

"Deloris," she said, "you wanna know why I'm laughing? Do you?"

Of course I did.

Without waiting for my answer, she said, "I went to tell him goodbye just now." She paused and began to laugh between words. "As I was standing there . . . he looked down at his lap. . . Naturally, I looked down too. . . And . . .

and . . . I couldn't believe what I saw. His . . . his . . . uh . . . his subpoena . . . it was—"

"It was what?"

"Ready to be served." She paused. "And no, and before you ask. Vera Dell was right. There wasn't any writing on it. Well, not any I could make out anyway."

CHAPTER FIVE

After making one more rest stop, we drove another thirty miles and came to a rise that overlooked Calvary Creek Valley. Baggett, a village that served as the home of the huge textile mill from which it got its name, occupied most of the valley. A red brick smokestack towered over the community, casting a long, dark shadow in the late afternoon over most of the area below. Some said one reason the mill owners built the smokestack so high was to symbolize their power and influence.

On the way into Baggett, we crossed over the railroad tracks that led to the mill and passed by a large billboard. It featured fading, side-by-side pictures of Baggett Mill and the smiling face of Baggett's mayor, the Honorable J. R. "Spot" Beebe. Several months before when Billy Joe Pratt and I had traveled to Baggett to interview a witness, he had described Mayor Beebe as having a "face that could launch a thousand gyps." Along the bottom of the billboard appeared the words: "If you lived in Baggett, you'd want to die here."

As we sped by the billboard, Dixie repeated the slogan and mumbled, "Truer words have never been spoken. That's because life's so miserable there and no one can ever save enough money to leave the durn place. So, you just wanna up and die."

Dixie's remark had the ring of truth about it, if what was said about Baggett Mill and the people who lived in the valley could be believed. Folks said the mill not only owned everything there was to own, but it also owned all the people. They said it even owned the dead and buried because the mill held title to the only cemetery in the valley—and of course, the funeral home.

Seeing as I was driving Dixie to Baggett, I wondered whether she called it home and, if she did, how she'd managed to get away from there herself. I had intended to ask her that before dropping her off, but I hadn't found the right opportunity. I rather doubted that she did. I couldn't imagine her being raised in a mill village, not as pretty and well-put together as she was. Like I heard somebody once say, she gave the word "gorgeous" a whole new meaning.

But that's not to say she didn't have her "technicalities," because she did. The terms "domineering," "self-centered," "quick tempered" fit her to a tee, but she had other characteristics beside these, good and bad.

Dixie hadn't spoken a word since she'd returned to the truck after the last stop. I looked at her out of the corner of my eye. "Dixie, you wanna tell me where you want me to take you to? We're just about to Baggett. You'll have to give me directions. About the only thing I know about the place is I sure wouldn't wanna live there. I don't care what that sign back yonder says."

Dixie uttered a deep, growling sound. It made me think for a second or two she might be having an attack of some kind.

"Tell you what, Deloris," she said.

"What?"

"I've changed my mind."

"Uh, say what now?" I said, a little taken aback.

"I've changed my mind."

What she said shouldn't have surprised me. If Billy Joe had told me once he'd told me a hundred times, Dixie could change her mind and her mood faster than the speed of light.

"Well," I said, "I reckon I'll have to let you out at the bus station."

"Baggett doesn't have bus stations. It's got bus stops, for your information. One for Trailways and one for

Greyhound. You catch one at the Bootle's Oil Station and get the other down the street at Eddie's Drive-In."

"Well, good. I'll take you to one of them. I don't have time to drive you all the way back home, doncha know."

She folded her arms. "Who said anything about you driving me back home? All I said was I've changed my mind. Isn't that what I said?"

"Yeah, okay. So, you don't wanna go back home. But I guess you still need me to take you to a bus stop. Which one you want, Greyhound or Trailways?"

"For what?"

"To take you wherever you're wanting to go to now."

"Who said I wanted a bus to take me someplace? I sure as heck didn't. You must be hearing things. Keep going."

Dixie now had me thoroughly confused. She didn't want to stay in Baggett. She didn't want to go home. She didn't want me to take her to catch a bus to somewhere else.

Once inside the town limits I slowed down when the speed limit dropped in a flash from 55 to 25 miles per hour. I glanced over at Dixie. "Lemme ask you something. What is it you want exactly? I need to get on my way to Texas. I've got lots to do there, doncha know."

"I said keep going," she said, without missing a beat. "I'm going there with you."

When she disclosed that little bit of information, I almost lost control of the truck and probably would have, had I been going faster. As it was, the left wheels hit the dirt shoulder of the road, making Dixie brace herself and cry out, "Watch where you're going, for Pete's sake!"

I steered the truck back onto the hardtop. "You say you wanna go to Texas with me? What brought that on all of a sudden?"

Just as I asked her a whistle blew, signaling a shift change at the mill. Scores of textile workers, swinging lunch pails, suddenly flooded the street just ahead as they came swarming through the main gate like a stirred-up colony of blue-clad yellow jackets. I slowed down to a crawl, creeping along and doing everything possible to avoid running over one.

After I got beyond the mill workers and realized Dixie hadn't answered my question, I repeated it.

Her answer? "I just do."

I started thinking about what the ramifications of taking her along might be. Nothing good came to mind, no matter how I sliced it. I needed to change her mind or, better yet, give her a reason to change her mind. I decided an appeal to her business relationship with Billy Joe would do the trick.

"But Dixie," I said, using a nice, even tone, "I don't know how long I'm gonna be out there. It might take me a good while to find this woman I'm looking for, doncha know. And that's assuming I even find her. Anyway, how long did you tell Billy Joe you'd be gone? I don't think he'd cotton to you laying out for more than a week, especially if he knew you'd be spending it with me on what might turn out to be a wild-goose chase."

"Billy Joe doesn't own me."

"No, but he employs you."

"Only if I let him."

"He depends on you. You're important to him."

"Will you just shut up and drive? I don't wanna hear all that."

I quit talking and drove on.

When I went by a sign on the edge of town telling me I was leaving Baggett and inviting me to return real soon, I renewed my effort to dissuade Dixie from accompanying me to Texas. "Don't you think whoever you were gonna visit there in Baggett, they're gonna be mighty disappointed you didn't come see them?"

"No," she said.

"Don't you think you at least oughtta call them and let them know you're not coming?"

She reached down and retrieved one of her romance magazines, ignoring my questions entirely.

I gave up. I had absolutely no idea about how to deal with the situation. I didn't know whether she really wanted to travel with me all the way to Texas or not. Being she was so quick to change her mind about things, I leaned toward it as being just a passing fancy.

I stopped at a four-way stop. "Look here, Dixie," I said, while waiting my turn to drive into the intersection, "I want a better answer to the question I asked you a while ago. I think I'm entitled to know that."

"How about this," she said in a quiet voice, dropping her magazine to the floorboard. "I've never in my life been to Texas. There, now. Does that satisfy you?"

"I dunno if it does or not."

"Well, you asked, and I told you."

She turned her back to me, shifted her weight onto her right buttock, and laid her head against the back of the seat. "Try to drive carefully and hush for a little while. I'm gonna try and get me some shuteye."

* * * * *

She slept for almost an hour. The moment she woke up, her first words were "Stop at the next filling station."

I figured as much. Her having to go to the bathroom all the time was getting to be a little aggravating. Now that she wanted to go all the way to Abilene with me meant I'd probably have to add at least another day to my driving on account of her needing to stop, it seemed like, every twenty or thirty minutes; and each time that happened, it wasn't always an in-and-out thing. Usually something that took me two or three minutes to do took her five or ten minutes, sometimes longer even.

Dixie got back aboard. "How far do you plan on driving today? I'm getting tired. This has to be the most uncomfortable seat I believe I have ever in my life sat down in. Another thing, I'm hungry. All I've eaten since this morning was a package of cheese crackers, a candy bar, and a grape soda that creepy client of yours bought me back there at that store."

I turned to answer her.

"Keep your eyes on the road," she ordered. "You've already run off of it one time, scaring the dickens out of me."

Ever since I'd picked her up that morning, whenever she had something to say it just about always was to complain. It was one complaint after another. If it wasn't "stop here," "don't talk," "keep your eyes on the road," "I'm hot," "you're letting too much breeze in here," "close the window, you're messing up my hair," "open the window," "you're going too fast," "you're going too slow," "watch out for that," it was "I don't like this," "I don't like that," "do this," and "do that." After driving all day and bone tired as I was, I had just about had enough of Dixie St. John. Beauty can take a person only so far, and hers had just about taken her to the end of the line.

When she began to complain again about how hard her seat was and for the first time about how its leather covering was sticking to her dress and fanny, I pulled off onto the shoulder of the highway and cut the motor.

"Why are we stopping out here in the middle of nowhere?" she snapped before giving me a hard look. "You better not be getting ready to try something. I'm warning you. If you so much as lay a finger on me, you sure better have good doctor insurance, cause you're sure gonna need it after I get through with you."

Before answering her, I sat for a moment to collect my thoughts. I sensed her staring daggers at me.

"Well?" she said, her hands balled into fist, "speak up."

I turned and faced her. She drew back and gave me an uneasy look.

"Dixie, I can't take any more of your bellyaching. I really can't. It's bad enough I have to stop for you to use the bathroom and then before I can even shift into high gear I have to stop for you to go again. But this ordering me around and bitching about anything and everything that doesn't go to suit you is getting a little old. I don't know what your problem is, but I've had it up to here," I said, drawing an imaginary line at my neck. "I sure as hell can't put up with all that all the way to Texas, I tell you that."

"Well, I've never!" she huffed.

"So, which is it, Greyhound or Trailways? Next town we come to, I'm dropping you off at one of them."

And with that, her lips started quivering and then she went to bawling. I hadn't counted on that kind of response. In any case, I tried not to pay her any attention. If anybody should've been crying, it should've been me. So, I just cranked up the truck and pulled out onto the highway, determined to look for a bus stop at the next town I came to.

Dixie must've carried on for about three or four minutes. The more she cried the phonier her crying sounded. I finally said to her, "I didn't know you could act."

She immediately stopped crying and went to sniffling. A minute or so later, she reached into her purse, withdrew a hankie, and blew her nose. Then, in a voice so gentle and sweet it could've belonged to a mother soothing a dying child, she said, "You wouldn't really drop me off at a bus stop, would you, Deloris?" She then reached over and rubbed the back of my neck.

Her action almost caused me to wreck my truck again.

I shifted my shoulders all around and she removed her hand. I glanced sideways at her. "What the heck are you trying to do, Dixie? Kill us both?"

She wiped her eyes with her handkerchief. "I must look a sight."

I didn't say anything. I wanted an answer about which bus stop she wanted me to take her to, not some comment that called for me to tell her how she happened to look at the moment. An apology from her for all her aggravation would've been nice, too.

As I came to the crest of a hill, something I couldn't quite make out moved toward the edge of the highway about a quarter-mile ahead. Drawing nearer, I realized it was a man and a woman. The man stood on the shoulder of the right-of-way while the woman sat on a large suitcase. Both had their thumbs in the air.

I slowed down.

"Just what do you think you're doing?" Dixie said, sitting straight up and leaning forward. "Surely, you're not thinking about giving them a ride, are you?"

"What? You don't want me to?"

"No, I most certainly do not. They could be escaped convicts, for all you know."

"What? With luggage?"

I stopped about twenty feet beyond the two.

The man ran up to the driver's side. "Hey, mister," he said, panting and smiling, "mind giving us a lift into the next town? We'd be much obliged."

I looked at Dixie. She shook her head "no."

I smiled at the man, a handsome young fellow about half my size or less. "Not a bit. Y'all throw your things into the back and climb on in. Door's not locked. It won't be the most comfortable place in the world to ride in, but it's a ride, doncha know."

"Yes, sir. We don't care. Just so you'll let us ride a ways with you." The man turned and waved for his partner to come on. "Thanks, Mister," he said. "Won't take us but a jiffy to get our stuff."

I watched in my side mirror as the man and the woman, a tiny little thing, each struggled to haul one large suitcase and two smaller pieces to my truck while cars and trucks zoomed by, kicking up loose gravel and blowing the woman's dark hair and flowered skirt around and about. I decided to get out and offer them help.

When I opened my door, Dixie said, "I think you're crazy to be doing this, you know."

I stepped to the ground and looked back at Dixie over my shoulder. "Maybe so. But when we come into the next town, I'm putting you out with them."

"That'll be the day," Dixie remarked.

* * * * *

I didn't have far to drive before reaching a place I could drop off my three passengers. As luck would have it, I spotted a Greyhound bus stop a mile or so into the next town. It operated out of a Standard Oil station that had an adjoining sandwich shop. I pulled into the parking lot and drove past a kerosene pump on my right and two gas pumps on my left. I came to a stop close to a Greyhound sign. Several white people stood off to the side smoking and talking, while three or four Negroes occupied a long bench along the outside wall of the station. The bench could easily have held nine or ten people.

"Why are you stopping here?" Dixie demanded.

I pointed to the dog in the bus sign. "I like dogs. And besides, this is where you're getting off."

I knocked on the wall behind me and yelled toward the open, inside entryway to my mobile office. "Okay, folks, y'all can get out now. We're where you can catch a Greyhound to take you where you need to go."

"Yes, sir," the man answered back.

I heard the back door of the truck grate open and then close. A moment later, the man popped up by my driver window. He brushed back his brown curly hair. "Can I ask you where y'all are headed, Mr. Meek?"

"Ain't no 'y'all.' Just me." I angled my head toward to Dixie. "She's getting out here too."

"No, I am not either," Dixie said matter-of-factly.

I gave her a dirty look. "The heck, you're not," I said in a raised voice.

The man's eyes widened, and his face went pink. "Sir, I didn't mean to—I hope we—"

"*I'm* going to Abilene, Texas," I said. "Why?"

His face brightened. "Really? You're really going to Abilene?"

I couldn't help noticing how happy he seemed when he learned where I was bound. "I gather you're going there too?" I said.

"No, sir. Not there, we're not. But we are going to Shreveport, which I think is on the way. To the Bayou Pickin' Parlor. It's close to Barksdale Air Force Base. Caters mostly to folks who love bluegrass music and such."

I eyed him cautiously. "You play bluegrass?"

"No, sir. You might say, we're 'the such,' me and Ginger are. We're a couple of ventriloquists. We've been booked for—"

"Ventriloquists?"

He grinned. "You might've heard of us? 'Wally and Ginger, Kody and Kuddles'?"

I shook my head. "Can't say I have. Which one are you? Kuddles?"

He laughed. "Oh, no, sir. I'm Wally. Wally Teal. That's not my real name, though, but it's the one I go by. My real name's Eli Fromberg."

His expression took on the humble and hopeful countenance of a criminal defendant, waiting to hear the judge pass sentence. "Sir, would you mind if we rode with you to Shreveport?" He quickly added, "I could help you some with the driving. I'm a good driver."

I considered his request. My first thought was it'd be interesting, even fun, to travel with a couple of ventriloquists, but then I remembered how I had imagined it'd be wonderful to travel with Dixie St. John, too. I'd been wrong about that, woefully so. On the other hand, I recognized Dixie was one of a kind.

"Okay, Wally," I said after thinking on it a little more. "You got y'all a ride to Shreveport. Go tell Ginger or Kuddles or whoever."

His big brown eyes danced as he burst into a smile that stretched all the way from one side of his face to the other. "Oh, thank you, Mr. Meek. Thank you, sir." He prepared to leave, but then hesitated for a moment. "It's Ginger, Mr. Meek. Ginger Childree. That's her real name. And could I say something else, sir?"

"Why sure. What?"

"You look kinda familiar for some reason. Something about your face."

"Really?" I said.

The next thing I knew he had gone around to the back of the truck and reloaded their suitcases.

While all that was happening, I turned to my other traveling companion. "I'm sorry, Dixie." I reached across her lap and unlatched the passenger-side door. "Out," I said as I pushed it open. "Wait there while I get your luggage."

Dixie sat frozen in place, arms crossed, both feet planted to the floorboard. I'd never seen her looking more defiant and more determined to have her way. "I'm not leaving this truck. You'd have to pull me out, and I warn you, if you so much as lay a finger on me, so help me—"

I remained calm despite the provocation. "Now, be sensible, Dixie," I said in a calm voice. "You're slowing me down what with that bladder problem you got. Aside from that, you're not the most enjoyable person in the world to travel with, doncha know. Nothing I do or say goes to please you. Another thing, I was only supposed to take you as far as Baggett. You remember that, don't you? So, will you please get outta my truck and go buy yourself a bus ticket home or wherever else you wanna go to?"

She didn't even look at me. She sat there, her head cocked to the side. "I'm not gonna do it, and that's that."

"All right, then. Just sit there."

I could almost feel my blood boiling. I decided to wait Dixie out. I went around to the back of the truck, removed her suitcase, and carried it inside, almost breaking my back in the process. I set it next to a counter where a cashier appeared to do double duty, selling tickets to bus passengers and taking in money from patrons of the restaurant.

An old gentleman who manned the cash register peered at me over his half-glasses. "Need a ticket, Mister?"

I shook my head. "Nah. This belongs to my soon-to-be ex-wife. She'll be in here in a few minutes. Right now, she's out in my truck, fixing her face." I winked at the man. "I can't believe I'm just about to be shed of her. Just can't believe it. No, sir."

The man scratched his cheek. "Yes, sir. Well, you ain't the first sent one back by Greyhound to her mama and daddy. Company oughtta have a special rate for 'em, I always say."

"I'm not sending her back to her parents. I'm sending her back to her third husband."

The man gave me a strange look. "You her fourth? Her fourth husband, you say?"

"Yeah, that's right. I kinda like them broke in, if you know what I mean."

The man's eyes widened. "Four husbands."

"Yeah. She thinks she's Liz Taylor." I looked around and then edged up close to the man. "Do me a favor," I said, speaking just above a whisper with a hand to my mouth. "Just make sure she makes the bus and send her as far as you can. Understand?"

The man laughed. "Do what I can."

I looked at my watch and approximated the time Dixie last had me stop for her personal comfort. I figured it'd be only a matter of ten or, at the most, twenty minutes that Dixie'd need to go again. Whenever that happened, I'd be on my way with Ginger and Wally. In the meantime, the smell of the onions and chili got to me. So, I grabbed me a couple of chilidogs prepared all the way and a pint of some ice-cold chocolate milk to wash them down with, paying for them in advance.

My plan worked like clockwork. Whenever Dixie rushed into the building on her way to the lady's room, I waved to Ginger and Wally. "Let's hightail it outta here."

And away we flew.

About a block down the road, I happened to look down and what did I see on the floor between the two front seats? Dixie's collection of romance magazines, that's what. The next time she saw me I figured she'd be mad, as the saying goes, as a cut snake on account of my driving off with her magazines. But I wasn't about to turn around and take them back to her.

* * * * *

With Ginger seated next to me and Wally sitting cross-legged on the floor in the open doorway behind the front seats, I drove to the outskirts of the town where I stopped to use a pay telephone. I wanted to call Billy Joe and tell him all that had happened.

When I gave him the news about leaving Dixie at the bus stop, he screamed at me. "You done what now? You left Dixie at some filling station in some hick town? Are you completely off your rocker?"

"Billy Joe," I said, "she didn't leave me with no choice. What would you have done? Anyway, you know how she can be. I'm not like you, willing to let her run all over me all the time. I'm telling you, it'd reached the point where I just had had enough of her and her selfish ways. Plus, I was having to stop all the durn time. I tell you one thing, she has certainly proved the truth of what somebody told me one time."

"Which is what?"

"*If you wanna learn about a person, take them on a trip somewhere.*"

Billy Joe offered no immediate comment, choosing to wait a little bit before saying anything more; and then when he did speak, it was to blame me for everything. "You shouldn't've agreed to take her with you in the first place. It's all your fault."

"All I agreed to was to take her to Baggett," I said. "And I didn't know nothing about her needing to go pee every fifteen or twenty miles."

There was another pause. "I guess you know, Deloris, what this means, doncha?"

"No. What?"

"You won't be able to call here no more, much less come around—at least, not when she's at work. And I'll tell you this. She'll probably kill you when she sees you, and there's not a jury in the whole wide world that'll convict her either, as good looking as she is and considering whatcha did to her. In short, you have played hell, buddy."

"Well, maybe so," I said. "But what's done's done. I'll call you tomorrow evening to let you know where I am and see if you've heard from her." I got ready to hang up. "One other thing."

"What?"

"I ran off with her romance magazines, but I didn't mean to."

Billy Joe swore a curse word. "Tell you one thing, Deloris. You better make sure you don't lose any of them, especially those that's got 'continueds' in them. Those are her favorites. She says they give her something to look forward to."

I promised Billy Joe I'd put them away in a safe place. "Oh, I almost forgot," I said. "Have you heard anything from Suffridge and them about suing me and the colonel's estate? They serve you yet?"

"No."

That was good news. "Maybe they won't sue after all, huh?"

"I wouldn't count on it, if I were you. You know the old saying, *A fool and his money are soon parted, especially if the fool's got a lawyer egging him on.*"

Finished with my conversation with Billy Joe, I returned to the truck. Wally chose to ride up front with me. We shot the breeze as we rode along. He seemed impressed that I was a lawyer. And like almost everyone I meet for the first time, he asked me what I'm doing with a girl name.

I learned from Wally that he and Ginger'd been a team for a little more than a year. They weren't married to each other and, except in a professional way, weren't interested in each other either. They had met in Columbia, South Carolina after Ginger caught Wally as he performed at the local Veteran's Hospital. He was stationed at Fort Jackson then as a clerk typist and did a ventriloquist act here and there to pick up a buck or two. She worked at the hospital as a volunteer when she wasn't performing with her dummy at children's birthday parties and the like.

They hit it off right from the start, he said; and as soon as the Army discharged him a few months later, they had some new dummies made, developed several comedy routines, and hired an agent.

But, he said, a problem quickly developed between them—one they never could have anticipated.

"What was it?" I asked.

Wally hung his head. "Something I don't really understand. Her dummy Kuddles doesn't like me, and my dummy Kody doesn't like her."

"That part of your act?" I asked.

"Started off that way. But then it started carrying over after the show, even when we'd put the dummies away in their cases."

"I never heard of such a thing."

"I know. I know. It's just plain weird." Wally blew out some breath and shook his head. "And the thing is I'm really very fond of Ginger. She's cute as a button, very bright, and talented. She can be as funny as Jack Benny and Bob Hope put together. Wait till you get to know her. You'll see. And she's got a heart as big as Texas. I mean, look at what she was doing when I met her. Doing volunteer work for veterans."

About a half-hour later we spied a motel or tourist court called "The Log-A-Zee." It consisted of fifteen or twenty white, red-roofed, log cabins each with its own stone chimney. The cabins sat nestled within a wood of chalk maples arranged in a semi-circle behind a larger building of similar design. The latter served as the office and restaurant. A highway sign by the concrete drive that ran behind the main building and in front of the cabins read, "Sleep like a log in our log cabins."

I looked forward to doing exactly that, as tired as I was.

The three of us checked in, with each of us having our own cabin. I offered to help Ginger with her things. She asked that I carry the cases in which she had put away Kuddles and her folding vent stand. As I walked with Ginger toward her cabin, we came up on Wally just as he set his suitcase down by his other two cases and went for his door key.

The moment I passed him, a muffled, female voice seemed to come from Ginger's dummy case. It sounded like somebody had said the word "bastard." And then came another muffled sound, this time seemingly from Wally's dummy case. I could almost swear I heard the word "bitch."

Startled, I looked at Ginger, a darling little woman with small boobs, auburn hair, gray eyes, pale white skin, and a cute fanny. "What the heck was that?" I said.

"Oh," she said. "That's just Kuddles and Kody. Don't pay them any mind. They get like this when they've been shut up all day."

"Hurry with that door, Ginger," came a voice seemingly from inside her dummy case, "it's hotter in here than a cathouse having a half-price sale."

* * * * *

About half-hour later, I strolled down the hill from my cabin to the Log-A-Zee's restaurant to meet Ginger and Wally for some pie and coffee. The owner had made a great effort to render the interior of the restaurant a memorable spot, having furnished its dining area with rustic log furniture and decorated its interior walls with photographs, old and new, of log cabins.

It took me a moment to spot my new traveling companions, so large a number of patrons crowded the dining area. Fortunately for me, they had saved me a seat. Their two dummies, Kuddles and Kody, sat at the table with them, their eyes closed. Like everyone else inside, they occupied chairs made with cane-weaved seats and backs. People at other tables kept gawking at the two, pointing, laughing, and making hushed comments. I stared at them myself, having only heard them "talk" but never having seen them.

Kuddles looked like the girl next door, with her curly blonde hair, big blue eyes, long eyelashes, and clear skin. Ginger had outfitted her that day in brown slacks and a white top.

Kody, on the other hand, wore blue jeans, a long-sleeve, black turtleneck shirt, white socks, and tennis shoes.

His appearance startled me. With the exception of having really big eyes and a galaxy of freckles, durn if he didn't look like a young me, with eyes, hair, and skin the color of mine. The only difference I could see? Unlike me, he had a trim body.

While I stood there marveling at the resemblance, Kuddles flashed open her eyes and looked straight at me. "Whatta you looking at?" The words seemed to leap from her mouth.

Startled, I jumped back. I hadn't expected the thing to "talk" to me, certainly not in a hateful way. "Oh, noth . . . nothing. I'm, uh . . . sorry," I managed to say. When I realized what I had done in speaking back to a huge doll, I felt like a fool.

Kuddles turned her head toward the other dummy. "Wake up, Kody."

Kody eyes blinked open and his head twisted right and left. "What? What's wrong?"

Kuddles cocked her head my way. "I believe we done found the guy who knocked up your mama."

Ginger smiled and patted Kuddles' head. "Now be nice, Kuddles. This kind gentleman is letting us ride to Shreveport with him."

Kuddles' head moved back and forth. "Okay, but if I were you I'd keep a close eye on him. I mean, look at him. If that big fella ain't Kody's old man, then I'll kiss Kody's acetone."

Kody's eyes seemed to grow larger and his mouth opened slightly. "But Kuddles, that can't be. You told me one time my daddy got himself cut all to pieces at a sawmill."

"I lied. That's him there, all right. Another thing, the only wood you got in you is that stick up your—"

Ginger smacked a hand to Kuddles' mouth. "Kuddles!" she exclaimed. "You know better than to say something like that."

Kuddles shook her head, freeing her mouth from Ginger's hand. "For goodness sake, Ginger, I was just talking about his control stick and trying to tell him, except for that, he wasn't made of wood, that's all."

In an eerie way, the sound of Kuddles' words, spoken as they were in a whiny, pitiful tone, kinda reminded me of Dixie when she had attempted to ingratiate herself with me after I told her I was dropping her off at the next bus stop. For a moment there, a tinge of guilt for leaving her like I did took hold of me; but only for a moment.

Wally tried to make light of the situation, thinking, I suppose, Kuddles had embarrassed me with her assertion of me having fathered Kody. Actually, it struck me as kinda funny.

"Kuddles is just joking with you and Kody, Mr. Meek," Wally said. He smiled across the table at Ginger and Kuddles. "Although I'll have to say, you and my buddy here, you do look alike."

Kody's head turned my way, appeared to stare at me for a moment, and his lips seemed to stretch into a frown. "I don't know how to take that," it seemed to say.

I laughed as I drew back my chair. "Me neither."

I decided to ignore the dummies and concentrate on the main purpose in being there—to order me a piece of pecan pie topped with a scoop of vanilla ice cream and then to engage in one of my favorite pastimes—eating.

CHAPTER SIX

As we proceeded toward Shreveport the following morning, Ginger and Wally went back into the office area of my truck to rehearse their routines. We reached the Shreveport vicinity about mid-afternoon, located the Bayou Pickin' Parlor, and checked into a nearby motel called "The Polk Inn."

At first, I assumed the owners named it after the former president and did not intend the name as a play on words. But later on, I began to wonder about that because the desk clerk, when we checked in, demanded we pay in advance and asked us, "How many hours y'all want your rooms for?" He frowned when we told him "all night."

The motel didn't look bad from the outside, but the inside told a different story. My room had a TV, but it was coin-operated, as was a bed-massage unit. A dresser with a cracked mirror sat to the left of a double bed whose chenille bedspread had a large hole burnt through the middle of it. The bathroom reeked of mildew, and no amount of fiddling with the flusher handle could stop the toilet from running. For me to shave, I'd have to stare into a penny-postcard size mirror that hung from a nail just above a rust-stained porcelain sink. The worst part about the room, though, was the whole time I spent in there I itched all over, leading me to promise myself I'd look for a doctor's office at the first opportunity and get me some shots.

We should not have stopped there, I realized too late. I cursed myself for not dropping Ginger and Wally off and continuing on my way to Abilene. The only reason I didn't do it was I'd promised them I'd catch their act that evening.

After I stored my luggage away in my room and killed a roach the size and color of an unshelled Brazil nut, I returned to my truck to meet Ginger and Wally. I had offered to take them to where they needed to go. Ginger got there ahead of Wally.

"How's your room, Ginger?" I said, scratching my back and then my thigh. "I feel like I've got things crawling all over me."

She laughed. "It's probably just your imagination. This place ain't the Log-A-Zee, that's for sure. But the price is right," she said.

She pointed to a large tent across the road. "Look yonder, Deloris. Is that a circus tent of some kind? I can't tell without my glasses."

I spotted a sign on the highway right-of-way near the tent.

I shook my head. "No, huh-uh. Sign there says it belongs to a revivalist. Calls himself Brother Jimmy Holcomb. Says services are at ten in the morning and seven in the evening. Wanna go?" I said, laughing. I intended the question as a joke.

She didn't answer right away, and when she did she sounded serious as can be. "Hmmm, might be interesting, sure nuff. Give me something to do. Besides, I've never been to a tent meeting before. How about you?"

"A few times, when I was a boy," I said. "Mama'd drag me off to one every now and then. You know, whenever one'd come to town, which was right often." I laughed. "No, she didn't do it for worship. She did it for entertainment. She liked to watch the holy rollers dance and kick about on the sawdust and hear them talk tongue whenever they'd get in the spirit."

"They'd really do that?" Ginger asked.

I laughed again. "You better believe it. But it always scared me, though, what with all them 'amens', 'hallelujahs', and 'praise the Lords' everybody kept yelling out. And the preacher, he'd be screaming and carrying on. One time I even saw one shimmy up a tent pole and preach from the top of it."

"Y'all been waiting on me long?" Wally said as he joined us.

"No," I said. "We just got here." I pointed to the tent. "Ginger wants to go there tomorrow. She wants to see the show. Wanna go with her?"

Wally shook his head. "No thanks. I'm with another crowd, you might say. Those that go to Shabbat services on Friday evenings."

"Aw, come on and go with her," I said. "You might learn something. Every now and then they'll have public confessions, and somebody'll get up and tell something pretty interesting such as confessing he's been sleeping with another man's wife or stole something. You know, stuff like that."

Wally smiled, and his face took on a serious look. "Public confession? Well, I tell you, Deloris, I've got every bit of respect in the world for the Christian religion. I really do. But there are some things about my religion that are definitely superior. And one of those is we don't make public confessions of our sins. Heck, it's bad enough God knows all about them."

Ginger stared up at me. "Deloris, please go with me. I really would like to have the experience. Please say you will." She laughed. "Never can tell, I might need a tutor. I wouldn't want to do the wrong thing."

Although I had no desire whatever to accompany her, I told her I'd go.

* * * * *

As honky-tonks go, The Bayou Pickin' Parlor wasn't too bad. I figured the Air Force base kept a close eye on the place and would be quick to put it off-limits at the first hint of trouble.

Finding Roda Anne

The red-brick building that housed the club struck me as once having been a supermarket. Large, glass windows and double doors between them fronted directly onto a sidewalk, and a large, paved parking lot formed a "U" around the building. Above the front door, a huge red, white, and blue sign advertised the club name while the two front windows invited passersby to partake of the bar, the pool tables, and the music, dancing, and entertainment inside.

I found an empty parking space across the street from the building. Two automobiles and a pickup sat in the left parking lot near the front. Since it was mid-afternoon, I hadn't anticipated anyone being there at that time except maybe a few barflies.

I was right. When Wally, Ginger, and I walked in, I glimpsed three men, sitting at the bar, each with a glass of beer keeping him happy while "Love's Gonna Live Here Again" by Buck Owens played on the juke box. One man sat several stools down from the other two, both of whom had red faces and porcine bodies. They appeared engaged in an argument of some kind until one spotted us as we came inside. After giving us the once-over, they resumed their argument. It concerned, as near as I could make out, whether Franklin Roosevelt had ordered the assassination of Huey Long in the 1930s.

The bartender, his back to us, stood bent over a cooler, refilling it with Pabst Blue Ribbon beer. When we caught the old man's eye, he walked from the lower end of the bar, a dishtowel draped over his shoulder and a pleasant smile on his face. "Howdy. Can I get y'all something other?" he said.

Wally jerked his thumb over his left shoulder, directing it up at the "Coming Attractions" board. The board occupied a space on the wall next to the women's restroom. Wally's and Ginger's picture with their pair of dummies filled the slot beside their names and show dates.

Above and below their picture were those of other performers, all clad in cowboy garb and none of whom I'd ever heard of before.

"No, sir," Wally said, offering the bartender a polite smile. "They told us to ask for Mr. Eddie Nolen. It's about tonight. That's us right there—Wally and Ginger, the ventriloquists."

The bartender glanced at the picture and back at Wally. Apparently satisfied Wally was the person he represented himself to be, the bartender flipped the towel off his shoulder and wiped his hands. "Wellsir, I see y'all, but where's Kody and Kuddles? Them's the ones folks'll come see."

"Oh, them?" Wally said with a slight laugh. "They're waiting outside."

"Yeah? I kinda liked to've seen them. I don't work the night shift," the bartender said. "Well, it don't matter, I don't reckon. Mr. Nolen, he told me to tell y'all when y'all got here to make y'all selves at home and for me to get y'all anything y'all might need. He's got the dressing room all set up. It's there in the back, right behind the stage. Just go through one of them doors yonder to get to the dance hall. Y'all'll see an exit door there in the back by the stage. Go through it and take a left. The dressing room, it'll be the first door on the right there. It's got a bathroom and everything—dressing table and so forth. There's a door out back, if y'all need to pull y'all's car around to unload something other."

"When do you suppose Mr. Nolen'll be here?" Wally said.

"Can't never tell, but I reckon he'll be here directly. Sometimes he's late coming, and sometimes he ain't. Just depends."

"Then do you know what time we go on tonight?"

The bartender cocked his head to the side and bit his lip. "Don't know exactly, but I expect it'd be sometime later on. Mr. Nolen, he likes to get the customers all lickered up before he wants the comedy folks do their thing. Says that makes folks laugh a whole lot more. Course, it also makes some of them get downright mean and start heckling. That's when they might have to bounce them right on outta here—you know, if they get too much outta hand. Don't want no trouble. No, sir. Don't want that. If the Air Force went and put the place on off-limits, that'd be all she wrote. And then, Mr. Nolen, he'd have to close up shop."

"But you do allow some heckling, if I understand you correctly," Ginger said. She didn't sound too happy about it.

"Yes, ma'am," the bartender said. "Some. Folks, way I understand it, they get a big kick from such goings on. Sometimes, them hecklers, they tell me, they'll try to outdo each other doing it and some of the things they say, they can be right funny,"

Ginger and Wally glanced at one another, each one appearing uneasy.

The bartender looked at me, his eyes narrowing. "Sir, you with them or what?"

Wally spoke before I could. "Yes. He's a lawyer."

The bartender drew back and glared at Wally. "You and her, y'all done brought a lawyer along? What, y'all think there's gonna be some kind of trouble?"

Wally laughed. "Oh, no. He's just a friend. In fact, he's coming to the show tonight, and we'd like for you to let him come in free of charge. He's helped us a whole lot, and we kinda owe him."

I stuck out my hand. "Deloris Meek. Please to meet you, Mr. . . ."

"Bacotte." He took my hand and tilted his head to the side as he looked at me. "That name you got, if I ain't mistaken, it sounds like a girl's name. Is it?"

I shook my head. "It's 'Deloris' with an 'I.' "

I turned to Wally. "Wally, you and Ginger go on to the dressing room. I'll pull my truck around back so we can unload your stuff." I gestured to Bacotte. "Is the door unlocked?"

"It's fixing to be," he said, staring at me and rubbing his chin. "I ain't never heard of no man ever being named Deloris before." He eyed me more closely. "You sure you ain't one of them sissy-breeches, Mister?"

The question drew the attention of the three patrons. They each one swiveled around to face me.

Just for the heck of it, I decided to mess with them.

"Who me?" I said. "Why, I'm anything but." I eased closer to Bacotte. "I betcha don't know where I might . . . you know, find me a friend for the evening?"

Bacotte reached around and scratched the back of his head. "Well, I might could."

The three customers kept their eyes trained on me.

"I figured you would," I said. "I don't care if she's old or young, fat or skinny. Just so long as she's frisky and legal—if you know what I mean." I gave him a wink. "I ain't picky."

Ginger and Wally looked at me like I had lost my mind.

* * * * *

After helping Ginger and Wally unload their stuff, I left them at the Bayou Pickin' Parlor, so they could get ready for their engagement that evening.

When I got back to my motel room, I telephoned Billy Joe to see if Bessie Phillips and her brothers had filed suit yet against Colonel Loomis' estate and to determine whether Billy Joe had heard anything from Dixie St. John. He answered "no" to both questions and again criticized me for leaving Dixie at the bus stop like I did. After learning he hadn't heard a word from or about Dixie, I started worrying about her and got down on myself pretty hard.

I returned to the Bayou Pickin' Parlor a little bit before nine o'clock that evening. Ginger had telephoned me at the Polk Inn to tell me they would be performing around nine-thirty or thereabouts. They expected a big crowd, she said.

Later on, when I presented myself at the entrance to the dance hall, a man sitting at a small table just inside the doorway asked me how many tickets I wanted. I told him my name and that I was supposed to have a free ticket. He leaned his chair back on its hind legs and studied me a second or two, his tongue planted against his cheek.

"Been expecting you," he said, setting his chair back down. "You the fella with a lady name."

"No, it's for a man."

He looked at me, tongue in cheek and nodded. "Uh-huh. Well, I hope you're happy with what all we done for you."

"I'm sure I will be," I answered.

The ticket seller motioned to another man who looked like a sideshow attraction at a cheap carnival. He stood about six-feet, eight inches tall, weighed I don't know how much, had neither neck nor hair but had biceps the size of a honeydew melon. The man straightened his tie and lumbered over to the ticket table. He folded his arms and looked me up and down, like he was getting ready to whip up on me or something.

"Atlas," the ticket man said with a wink, "this here's that Deloris fella we've been saving that table for in Section C. Wanna show him where it is for me?"

Atlas grumbled something I couldn't quite make out and, with a sneer and a head motion, signaled me to follow him into the dance hall, a place so smoke laden and noise filled I could barely breathe or hear. Once inside, he bullied himself ahead onto the dance floor, cutting a path for us through the crowd, knocking aside men and women—he didn't care which. No one offered any resistance or offered any complaint. About forty or fifty feet in, we came to a small, round table situated in a dark, out-of-the-way corner but offering a good view of the stage.

I'd hardly sat down when a thin-waist man with brown kinky hair, a gold tooth, and broad shoulders wandered over to my table arm-in-arm with a female companion. The latter, a red-headed, well-built, made-up, buxom woman of the floozy variety, batted her mascara-laden blue eyes at me as the man assisted her with a chair next to me. I put her age at somewhere between forty-five and fifty and his at about thirty or so. An eye-burning scent of cheap perfume clung to her like stink on a skunk, as the saying goes.

"And who might you be, old sport?" the male said as he took a chair opposite me.

Halfway standing, I extended my hand. "Name's Deloris. Deloris Meek."

He took my hand. It had the soft feel of a girl. That made me feel kinda ooky inside.

"Grover Hale," he said above the din of the dance hall.

I jerked my hand away, startled at what I understood him to say. "Did you just tell me to go to Hell?"

The woman laughed. "Honey, everybody says that whenever they hear his name for the first time. No, it's Grover Hale. H-a-l-e, not H-e-l-l."

"But is your name really Deloris?" the woman said. "I'm guessing your mama wanted a little girl? How sweet to name you that. Don't you think so, Grover?"

"It's spelled with an 'I,' " I said. "If it's for a girl, it'd be with an 'E,' doncha know."

"Who cares?" the woman said with a shrug. " 'E,' 'I,' it's still Deloris, of course. Oh, just listen to me, Grover, I just made a rhyme. Deloris, of course, of course, of course—"

Grover waved at his companion. "Oh, silly. Quit that." He then reached across the table and patted the top of her hand. "This is—how shall I say it?—the 'friend' you told Mr. Becotte you wanted him to get you for this evening. She's the best I could do on such short notice."

The woman leaned toward me. "Just call me 'Olive,' honey, and I'm all yours—right down to the pit, you might say."

"What are you talking about?" I said, thoroughly confused.

Rather than answer me, Olive just smiled.

"You have a middle name, don't you, Deloris?" Grover asked.

I slid my chair away from Olive a couple of inches, but the perfume followed me like a dog chasing a bicycle. "Yeah. It's Ursel."

"Ursel?" He grimaced. "I don't think I've ever heard that name before. Have you, Olive? You sure it's a name, Mr. Meek?"

I didn't reply.

Grover rubbed his chin. "Let's see. Your initials, then, are 'D' for Deloris, 'U' for Ursel, and 'M' for Meek. D-U-M. Dum. You're not dumb are you, Mr. Meek?"

"Some folks might think I am," I said.

"People," Grover declared, shaking his head.

"Anyway," he continued on, "Olive and I, we're supposed to make you feel really, really welcomed to the Bayou Pickin' Parlor, Mr. Meek—or may I call you Deloris, Deloris? Hmmmmm?"

I began to feel very uncomfortable. He talked a little too effeminate for my liking. "Look, y'all," I said, "I just come here to watch the show. That's all."

Grover and Olive looked at each other and frowned.

"Why, Deloris," said Grover, "that's what we wanna do too—watch the show. Whatever gave you the idea we didn't? We're in no hurry. No hurry at all. I really, really like ventriloquists. I just love Charlie McCarthy."

"I like Mortimer Snerd better'n him," Olive said. "He's so . . . so dumb." She smiled sweetly at me. "But I kinda like them dumb. The dumber the better. And your initials, they spell DUM. How cute."

"Wally and Ginger, they're friends of mine, doncha know," I said in an attempt to explain my presence and clear up any misunderstanding. "They asked me to—"

"My, my," said Olive. "What do you know about that, Grover? Deloris has friends in show biz. I'm impressed."

"Which ones are his friends?" Grover said with a slight laugh. "I certainly hope it's not the dummies. Oh, please tell us it's not the dummies, Deloris."

"Now, Grover," Olive said, shaking a finger, "there's no need for you to be impolite."

"I'm just kidding him, for goodness sake," Grover said in a huff. "You will forgive me, won't you, Deloris, if I offended you?"

A waiter appeared at that moment to take our drink orders. "Just bring me a ginger ale," I said.

Olive and Grover both ordered champagne and hors d'oeuvres, mainly shrimp cocktails and cheese balls.

"Should I run a tab?" the waiter asked, his pen poised above his order pad.

"Oh, by all means. Please do," Olive said before I could say anything.

As soon as the waiter returned with my ginger ale, I excused myself and went and stood against the wall to watch folks dance as I waited for the floorshow to begin. Grover and Olive remained at the table, chitchatting and enjoying their champagne and stuff, which they kept re-ordering. Every now and then, they'd glance back at me, make a face at each other, and double over in laughter.

Around nine-thirty, the lights in the dance hall dimmed and a spotlight hit the stage, lighting the area around the microphone. A handsome man with wavy black hair and dressed in a navy-blue suit, white shirt, and regimental tie came into the light. He motioned for the crowd to quiet down. Bending forward, he spoke into the mike. "Ladies and gentlemen, welcome to the Bayou Pickin' Parlor. I'm Eddie Nolen, owner and general manager. Before we introduce our first act for this evening, let's give a round of applause for the Peanut Pickers, our band tonight. They come to us all the way from the Wiregrass country of South Alabama."

Once the applause died down, he spoke again. "And now, without further ado, it is my pleasure to introduce to you, an act fresh off the nightclub circuit in the Northeast, Ginger and Wally with their little friends Kuddles and Kody. Come on up here, folks. Let's give them a big hand, Shreveport."

Ginger and Wally rushed into a circle of light with their dummies and vent stands. The first voice was that of Kuddles. "Hey, Nolen. Hold up a minute before you go bounding off. What's this crap about a nightclub circuit in the Northeast? Northeast what? Yazoo City? Why there ain't a nightclub within five hundred miles of the place. Billy clubs, yeah, but ain't no nightclubs there I've seen."

I retook my seat as Nolen waved a friendly goodbye and left the stage. Olive welcomed me back with a blown smooch and a "Hey, Darling." I could tell she was feeling her champagne.

Olive elbowed me. "Deloris, honey, that boy dummy, I swear he's your spitting image. Don't you think so, Grover?"

"I most certainly do." He laughed. "My, my, Deloris, just what have you been up to? Don't tell me you've—how shall I say it?—been playing with dolls?"

I paid them no mind and settled back in my chair to watch the act.

Ginger and Wally opened their act with an old routine drawn from Wally's experience in the Army—which, as it turned out, proved a mistake, particularly after Wally mentioned having served in the Army. The crowd consisted mostly of Air Force personnel, and any mention of the Army riled them up. Wally soon became the target of several hecklers, so much so he could hardly say either his lines or Kody's. Ginger fared no better. The only one who seemed immune from insult was Kuddles.

At one point, a heckler sitting near the front yelled out, "Hey, Wally, you know why they call an Army guy a 'G.I.'? Stands for 'gastrointestinal.' Other words, it means y'all are full of it."

The remark brought much laughter, which only encouraged the heckler.

As this was going on, a hand brushed my knee. I slapped it away and said to the person nearest me, "Olive, I swear, if you do that one more time—"

"Do what?" Olive said, appearing very much offended.

"You know what. Don't you touch me like that again. I am not interested. Got that?"

She got it, all right. She gave me a look that could kill, hopped her chair a foot or so away from me, and huffed. "I didn't mean to touch you. I was merely trying to find my napkin. You jumped—"

I dismissed Olive with a wave of the hand. "Yeah, right."

The heckler was still at it. "We're confused here. Your dummy moves his lips whenever *you* talk."

Wally now seemed thoroughly frustrated. He yelled back at his tormentor, "Hey, buddy, would you do me a favor and stand up a second?" He motioned toward the back of the dance hall. "Could we have some light down front?"

The beam of the spotlight widened to reveal a bald, burly man decked out in blue jeans and a matching jacket. He stood, facing the stage and grinning, as the saying goes, "like a mule eating briers."

Wally leveled a finger at the man. "Look there, everybody. It's what proctologists the world over have been looking for—the perfect asshole."

And with that, all hell broke loose. A chair came soaring onto the stage, knocking over Kody's vent stand and sending both Wally and Kody tumbling toward Ginger and Kuddles. Ginger screamed as she and Kuddles followed them to the floor. Wally attempted to pull himself up; but the man who'd been doing most of the harassing, now on stage, jumped on top of Wally, hit him full-fisted in the face, reached for Kody, and began flogging Wally with the little fella.

I figured I'd better do something to help poor Wally out, so I went racing toward the stage. Just as I cleared the last step, the man swung Kody back to hit Wally again and Kody's head came flying off. It hit me right between the eyes, knocking me down the steps. When I attempted to get back on my feet, who should be standing over me and looking down at me but Olive and Grover. I kinda raised myself up on one elbow and, attempting a smile, offered them my hand.

Instead of taking hold of it, Olive laid the sharp point of a shoe into me and said, "If there's one thing I believe in, it's kicking a man when he's down."

"Me, too," Grover said.

And with that, they both went to stomping me in the chest and kicking me in the back, her harder than him. They let me have it in the gut, in the groin—anywhere they had a clear shot. They even tried kicking me in the head, except I'd managed to cover it up with my arms and hands—though some glancing blows got through anyhow, mostly to the back of my head and neck and at least one to the jaw.

I think they would have killed me had it not been for Atlas. He pushed them off me and snarled, "Now, y'all get the hell out, unless you wanna piece of me."

Olive snickered and answered him back. "Honey, I don't know about Grover, but I'd love that. Where you wanna meet at? How about the Polk Inn?"

Atlas, his fist raised, feigned a charged toward the two, making them turn and scurry away as fast as their feet would haul them.

With Olive and Grover rushing toward the back exit, Atlas lifted me from the floor, shaking his head. "I just knew you'd be trouble the moment I saw you. I can spot troublemakers a mile away. Yes, sir. I just knew it. There's just something about you. Yes, sir. There sure is."

As I brushed myself off and made sure I was still in one piece, Atlas spun around and walked away, mumbling to himself before I could offer him my thanks.

The area around the stage lay in shambles. Kody had been torn asunder, his head and control stick resting on the floor by the steps and his little body crumpled on stage. Ginger and Kuddles survived the melee intact, but poor Wally had to be taken to the emergency room, beat up as he was and bleeding from his nose and mouth.

I didn't feel none too good myself. I hurt just about all over and could imagine what the pain would be like the next morning once the injuries I suffered at the feet of Olive and Grover settled in.

Nolen apologized to Ginger, saying nothing like that had ever happened in his place before and he hoped neither she nor Wally would say anything to the Air Force about it. He peeled off five one-hundred-dollar bills from a wad he drew from his pocket and gave them to her, telling her that she and Wally need not return the next evening—

not that Wally would be able to, not from the looks of him, to say nothing of Kody. Nolen also promised to take care of Wally's medical bills and to have Wally's and Ginger's equipment and other things brought to the motel the next morning.

    I got ready to leave with Ginger when the waiter came up to me. "Excuse me, sir," he said, "but you owe us $55.30, plus a twenty-percent service charge."

    "For just a ginger ale?" I said.

    "No, sir," he said. "For that and all the stuff your friends ordered too."

CHAPTER SEVEN

The owner of the Bayou Pickin' Parlor had Atlas bring Wally from the hospital to the motel after the doctors got done with him. I understood he had a broken nose, busted lips, a sprained right wrist, and numerous bruises about his face, neck, and upper body. There was no telling when he'd be able to perform again as a ventriloquist, particularly since poor Kody now had been beheaded and would need almost a complete make-over.

I got up early the next morning and called Wally's room, but I couldn't rouse him. I figured the doctors must've given him a powerful sedative for him not to answer the phone—either that or he'd passed.

When I looked into the mirror at myself, I couldn't believe all the bruises and abrasions I had about my neck and face. As for my body and limbs, they looked about the same. The pain that accompanied my injuries was something else again. It hurt me to walk, to sit, to lie down, to stand up, to breathe—to do everything. I knew there was no way I could resume my trip toward Abilene right then. Another thing, I kept remembering about how Dixie had tried to tell me not to pick up Ginger and Wally that day. Had I listened to her, I'd probably been in Abilene already, even after having to put up with her frequent nature calls.

I telephoned Billy Joe to tell him what all had happened. I got no sympathy from him whatsoever. He said something about payback being hell. I said, "Payback for what?"

He said, "For leaving Dixie, that's what. You shouldn't've done it, and you know you shouldn't've done it. But then, you ain't one who's been gifted with even a modicum of good sense."

I ignored the cut and asked him if he had heard from her yet. He said he hadn't and was beginning to get very concerned about her. When he lit into me some more about Dixie, I hung up on him. I didn't feel like jawing with him anymore about it. I had my own troubles.

A little after nine o'clock Ginger came and stood outside my door to inquire whether I still would go with her to the tent revival across from the motel. It was to start within the hour. I tried to beg off, telling her I really didn't feel like I could even make it across the highway, I hurt so badly.

She wouldn't take no for an answer. "Deloris," she said, "you're gonna hurt no matter where you are or might be doing. You might as well be doing something that could take your mind off how you're feeling, if only for a little while. Come on and go with me, please."

I relented and agreed to accompany her.

While Ginger waited outside my door, I took me another Goody Headache Powder and donned a white Banlon pullover, a pair of tan slacks, and a blue sport coat, although it near about killed me to put it all on. I didn't bother to shave. I couldn't have, even if I had wanted to. It hurt like the dickens for me to raise my arms or to touch my face—really to do anything that required movement.

With Ginger's assistance, I somehow managed to get across the highway. She guided me into the tent and sat me down on the back row. The effort made me feel even worse. In fact, I worried I'd fall apart any second.

No sooner than Ginger had me seated she took off only to return about five minutes later, carrying Kuddles. Ginger took an end seat and sat Kuddles on her lap.

"Hey, Deloris," Kuddles appeared to whisper, "you here for the healing service?"

"Quit it, Ginger," I said. "It hurts me to laugh."

"Don't look at me," Ginger said. "Kuddles said that."

Kuddles bumped against my shoulder. "You didn't answer my question. I think you come to the right place, though. You look like you're in need of divine healing." There came a pause. "But then, you looked like that before your buddies whipped your sorry ass."

"Kuddles!" Ginger exclaimed. "Now quit that. You're in church."

Kuddles' head turned first to the right and then to the left. "I don't know about you, sister, but I'm in a tent."

I leaned over to Ginger. "Please, make her stop," I said in a whisper. "I've done told you it hurts when I laugh—really."

Ginger laughed and, mumbling a complaint in Kuddles' voice, removed her hand from Kuddles' back.

I probably should have allowed Ginger to continue because now all I could think about was the hard, metal chair I was sitting on. The chair, as were all the rest, was of the fold-up, undersized-seat kind that funeral homes usually placed in front of caskets. The design of the chair, whether intentional or not, served to discourage long periods of sitting, especially for big-ass people like me. I sat there in terrible pain and keenly aware that, to my further discomfort, my butt overlapped the chair seat.

If that wasn't enough misery, the sawdust that covered most of the ground under the tent, with its woodchip odor mixed with the scent of canvas, not only gave the place its own special ambience, it activated my allergies, causing me to sneeze my head off. The sneezes, in turn, wrought havoc on my rib cage. After awhile, the sneezing ended but not the pains in my chest and elsewhere.

A pianist, an elderly lady with a pleasant face and blue hair, ran through a selection of upbeat redemption songs as the time for the service approached. People sauntered into the tent, pausing at its entrance before taking seats near the front. When they passed by us, several did double-takes, no doubt to confirm their sighting of a small woman holding, what to them, appeared to be a large doll. Some folks shook their heads, disgusted like, while others laughed or smiled.

By the time Brother Jimmy Holcomb, a tall, slender man in a double-breasted, navy-blue suit, white shirt, and red tie, came on stage to begin the service, I had counted forty-three adults inside the tent, which I didn't think was too bad for a weekday morning. Women and the elderly made up most of the worshipers, although I spotted one young man in a wheelchair. Five or six small children, every one of them misbehaving, and a baby, who didn't stop squalling until its mama flipped out a breast and stuck it into the baby's mouth, filled out the rest of the congregation.

After singing "Jesus on the Main Line" for a good ten minutes, Brother Holcomb, backed up by a trio of middle-age women with long hair, long necks, long skirts, and short on makeup, commenced his sermon. I figured he'd preach on one of two subjects: either the fires of Hell or money. He chose the latter, using as the basis of his sermon the story of the rich young man found in *Mark* 10:17-22 and the story of the widow's mite found in *Luke* 21:2-4.

"You know," Brother Holcomb said, "some churches say you oughtta tithe—give the Lord ten percent of your total income. Notice I said *total income.* I didn't say *net income.* No, uh-uh. That ten percent, it comes off the top—whatcha get before taxes and before all that other stuff is taken out. But I'm here to tell you this morning, tithing ain't the way to go. No, siree. Tithing is Old Testament stuff. The New Testament says to give it all. Ain't that what Jesus told the rich young fella to do with his riches, his money? *Go sell everything,* He told him, *and give the proceeds to the poor.* "

Brother Holcomb paused long enough to take him a sip of water.

"So, what am I telling you to do? Give it all, brother. Give it all, sister. Just like that poor widow woman done. She give it all. And if you wanna be right with the Lord, you'll have to give it all your own self."

I notice people all around me starting to squirm and look at one another.

"Now I know what a lot of you are thinking right now. You're saying to yourself, *I need my money for me and mine.* But I have to ask this question. Do y'all need it more than the Lord does? Well, what about it?"

He paused again.

"Lemme tell you something. What will be the consequence if you give it all—and everything you do has consequences; don't you fool yourself. Just think what's in store for you later on if you do the right thing and give it all—and that 'later on' just could be tonight or tomorrow morning. Why, you might suffer a heart attack or a stroke or die in a car wreck or something—you don't know. If that happened to you, wouldn't you wanna've invested in a ticket to ride that glory train way on up to Heaven where you'll see crystal rivers and golden streets; live in hilltop mansions surrounded by green pastures; join hands with martyred saints and listen to angel choirs; and enjoy family reunions and rejoin old friends who've gone on before?"

Citing *1st Corinthians* 15:42-54, he spoke of the resurrected dead and of their new imperishable bodies. "Yes, my friends," he cried out in a broken voice, "you will see little babies who were born dead, cooing and crawling; folks who were once crippled, walking and running; people who were once blind, looking and seeing; and those who were dumb, singing and praising God, Amen."

I noticed Ginger perked up when Brother Holcomb mentioned the dumb.

Brother Holcomb went on. "But ain't none of that gonna happen to you if you rob the Lord of what is rightfully His, especially if you take it and spend it on whiskey and cards and whatnot. Whatcha mean, preacher, by that word 'whatnot'? I'm talking about second helpings at the supper table, fancy clothes—stuff like that. And yes, ladies, I'm talking also about all that makeup you smear on your face, a face that's gonna perish someday just like the rest of your body's gonna do. Heck fire, it just may be doing that right this very minute no matter what you've been doing to it."

Brother Holcomb wound down about ten minutes later and, as I fully expected, announced an offertory, striking while the iron was hot, as it were. Instead of using either plates or baskets for worshippers to put their money in, he had his ushers pass around big glass jars that might've contained pickled cucumbers at one time. I figured he used these so people could see what other folks had given, perhaps to shame them into giving at least as much or more. More than one trembling hand and anguished face passed a collection jar to another.

When the jar reached Ginger, she took it and laid it in Kuddles' lap. Kuddles leaned to one side and then to the other, as if examining the jar and, while so engaged, appeared to utter something that sounded like "Looky there, Ginger, at all that money. You thinking what I'm thinking?"

I got the impression Kuddles would have reached into the jar and pulled out a wad of money if able to do so. I laughed but for only a second or two because one of ushers caught my attention by clearing his throat and inclining his head in Kuddles' direction. I assumed he wanted me to take the jar from Ginger and hand it to the person sitting next to me, which I did after making a small contribution. The clinking sound my quarter made when it struck the glass told of its form, prompting a look of disgust from the usher.

After the ushers collected all of the jars and laid them before the pulpit, Brother Holcomb offered a prayer that was more of a sermon meant for human ears than a petition directed to the Almighty. He followed it with an invitation to those who sensed the Lord calling them to meet him down front during the singing of the final hymn.

While the congregation sang "Just as I Am," while Brother Holcomb, with tears streaming down his face, begged everyone "to accept the free gift of salvation," and while a number of worshipers slipped into the aisle to go join Brother Holcomb, a sharp jab to my ribs caught my attention.

It was Ginger.

"Don't look now," she said, "but I believe this is the end of our act."

"What?" I said.

She glanced over at the aisle and then at Kuddles. "She wants me to take her down front."

"Say what now?" I said, startled.

Without another word, Ginger rose from her seat and, with Kuddles on her hip, made her way toward the open arms of Brother Jimmy Holcomb—and Jesus.

* * * * *

When the service ended and Ginger came back, I returned to my motel room, took me some more headache powder, and fell onto the bed after removing only my coat and shoes. I went to sleep almost immediately. I don't know how long I slept. I woke up at the sound of a knock on my door.

Although it was quite a struggle for me to do, I lifted myself out of bed and half-walked and half-stumbled in sox feet to the door. "Who is it?" I asked.

"It's me," said a familiar voice.

I opened the door, and there stood Ginger, holding Kuddles.

"Tell him, Kuddles," Ginger said, smiling.

Kuddles smiled too. "Deloris, me and Ginger, we've just checked out. We're moving across the way into one of Brother Holcomb's travel trailers."

"Into one of Brother Holcomb's travel trailers? Did I hear you right, Ginger?"

"I'm the one talking to you. Not her," Kuddles appeared to say, sneering like. "I'm joining Brother Holcomb's ministry, and I'm gonna be an evangelist. How's that grab you?"

I stood there in the doorway, stunned by what had just been said. "Uh, tell me that again?"

"Yeah. Brother Holcomb wants me to join his ministry, and Ginger's letting me do it. Ain't that right, Ginger?"

Ginger withdrew her hand from inside Kuddles and reached for my arm. "What else could I do? Kuddles told me last night, Deloris, she no longer wanted any part of the act—not after what happened to Kody, she didn't."

Ginger licked her lips as she looked at me. "I think her problem, Deloris, is she's scared to go back into nightclubs again. That awful thing last night really, really got to her. And if she wants to give the ministry a try, I mean, what can I do about it?"

I told myself that this had to be the wackiest conversation I had ever had anywhere with anyone at anytime about anything. And that included the one I had with the guy who wanted me to bring a lawsuit against the city to have one-way streets declared unconstitutional on equal protection grounds. He maintained equal treatment under the law required all public streets to allow vehicular traffic to flow both ways. While he had a point, he didn't have the money to pay me to promote it.

Before I could respond, Brother Jimmy Holcomb sidled up beside Ginger, a well-worn Bible in his hand. Had I not seen him earlier, I would've guessed him to be a member of a gospel quartet, what with his expensive suit, heavily ringed fingers, and dyed black hair.

"The Lord bless you, friend," he said, extending a hand in Christian fellowship.

After shaking his hand, I invited them in. "I apologize for the room." I pointed at a chair over which I had thrown my coat. "You can sit there, Reverend, if you don't mind the coat, and watch out for my shoes there. Ginger, you take that other chair. I'll just sit here," I said, easing myself down onto my unmade bed.

After a minute or two of small talk, I said, "So, Reverend, what can I do for you, sir?"

Holcomb smiled. "You can't do nothing for me, Brother Meek, but Christ can, and He has. But that ain't why I come over to talk to you. What I wanna tell you is Sister Ginger and Sister Kuddles—"

Sister Kuddles? I thought.

"—they'll be joining my ministry."

"Yeah," I said. "Ginger . . . well, Kuddles just told me."

An even bigger smile spread across Holcomb's face. "I plan on using Sister Kuddles in my children's ministry, and she'll be doing her very first sermon tonight, Lord willing. We'd love to have you come, if you feel like you can make it."

"I don't really feel up to it, Reverend. I still hurt all—"

Ginger broke in. "Deloris, please. It'd mean so much to Kuddles and me for you to be there—to hear her first sermon and all. You could leave after she gets through. Couldn't he, Brother Holcomb?"

"Why certainly," Holcomb said. "We don't never keep nobody from coming, and we don't never keep nobody from leaving. Free choice and free will. That's what I preach, amen. I don't preach none of that predestination stuff."

"Come on and come, Deloris," Ginger begged.

Then Ginger spoke as Kuddles. "Yeah, please, Deloris. Pretty please."

"Okay," I said. "But I'm just coming to hear Kuddles, and then I'm leaving. I wanna try and go to bed early. I'm planning on heading out early tomorrow morning, and I do mean early, no matter how badly I hurt."

Ginger poked out her lips. "You were gonna leave without telling me goodbye?"

"No, but then I didn't know about all this—your joining up with Brother Holcomb and checking outta the motel."

She got up from her chair, wrapped her arms around my shoulders, and hugged me tight. "Thank you, Deloris. You've been a God-send," she said, wiping her eyes. "You gonna tell Wally?"

"That I'm leaving in the morning?"

"No, about me."

"You don't think you oughtta tell him yourself?"

"I couldn't bear it. Please do it for me, Deloris. Please."

I didn't wanna do it, but I told her I would anyway.

I reached for my wallet, withdrew a business card, and handed it to her. "Here, Ginger. Take this. If y'all're ever back east and you need me, call me at the number listed there. It's really Kingry Insurance, but they'll get in touch with me for you."

After a word of prayer in which Brother Holcomb asked the Lord to bless Kuddles' ministry and to heal Wally and me, my visitors left. The reverend said nothing about making poor Kody whole again.

* * * * *

That evening I stopped by Wally's room before going over to Brother Holcomb's tent. I figured it best to tell him first about my plans before saying anything about Ginger's.

When I told him I had to move on early the next morning, he said he understood and flopped down on his bed.

Although Wally still had trouble talking because of his broken nose and swollen lips and moved around kinda tentative like, he otherwise seemed to be doing all right and able to handle things—that is, until I told him my other news, the news about what Ginger had decided to do.

His reaction surprised me—not for being upset but for whom he blamed.

"That's Kuddles' doing," he said. "She's never liked me, the little bitch."

"Well, Wally, you sure it's Kuddles?" I said, amazed at his odd disclosure.

"Hell yes, I'm sure. You've heard how she talks to me. And you oughtta hear the things Kody told me she's said about me."

"Things Kody told you?" I said.

"Right."

I closed my eyes and shook my head sideways. "Okay then. If Kody told you that, Wally, I guess Kuddles said it all right. Kody wouldn't lie, I don't guess."

"Hell no, he wouldn't. Not to me, he wouldn't, the poor little guy."

Wally then went into a tirade, cursing Kuddles and calling her all kinds of bad names.

After seeing him carry on like that, I figured there wasn't any use in my hanging around any longer. It finally dawned on me that the drugs they'd given him to lessen his pain might've made him a tad loonier.

I reached for the doorknob. "Wally, I gotta go. Before I do, is there anything I can get for you or anything you want me to do for you? I'm planning on leaving here as early tomorrow morning as I can."

Instead of answering me, Wally flipped over onto his other side and started crying.

"What am I gonna do? What am I gonna do?" he kept saying as I closed the door behind me.

Finding Roda Anne

I checked on my truck, walking around it to make sure I'd locked the doors and the tires hadn't gone flat. Everything appeared okay, and I strode on over to the edge of the highway. While I waited to cross over, I glanced at the revival tent on the other side of the road. I noticed Brother Holcomb had installed an additional sign. It read, "Come hear the dumb speak as Sister Kuddles brings the Word to our little children."

Once on the other side of the highway, I joined those who now made their way into Brother Holcomb's tent. The evening flock appeared larger and younger than the one at the morning service. Only one seat remained on the back row, and I quickly grabbed it.

I sat down by a man with a stubby chin and no teeth. His lips as were his cheeks maintained a constant motion, his lips poking in and out and his cheeks sunken one moment and full the next.

I greeted him with a slight nod.

He looked me over. "You here for the same reason I come, Mister?"

"And what reason is that?"

"Brother Holcomb, he's gonna heal some dumb woman named 'Sister Kuddles' tonight. And after he gets done doin' it, she's gonna stand up right up there on that stage yonder and preach the Gospel. Least, that's what somebody told Mr. Cousineau down there at the bait shop and what he told my cousin—the one we all call 'Pooter.'"

"Pooter, you say?"

"Yes, sir. You know him?"

"No, can't say I do."

"He's a nice fella, but you can't depend on him none. Lies, too, and he'll do it when the truth would make do. He's still a nice fella, though. He's supposed to come tonight, he told me. Done should've been here. But his mama says he'll be late for his own funeral." He hushed for a moment as he stood partway up to take a quick look-see down front. "I sure hope he ain't been lyin' about what's supposed to happen here tonight. I took off work to come see it. It'd be somethin' to tell your grandchillrens about—makin' somebody talk what ain't never talked before. Know what I mean?"

The music started when the blue-haired piano player of the morning service, now joined by an elderly blind man at a Hammond Organ, began playing "Leaning on the Everlasting Arms." She followed that with "Love Lifted Me." After the fourth or fifth song, Brother Holcomb and Ginger walked out onto the stage. Brother Holcomb took hold of the microphone and welcomed everyone and asked everybody to bow their heads while he gave an invocation. That done, he led us all in a hymn-singing that got the crowd all worked up and loose.

The man sitting next to me could not have carried a tune even if they'd given him a shopping cart to carry it in; but he gave it his best effort. Every now and then he'd stand and stretch his neck to peer toward the stage. Finally, he turned to me and said, "Mister, I ain't seen nobody but that little woman up there with the reverend. Reckon that's Sister Kuddles—the one what's gonna get healed and start talkin' for the first time in her whole life? She don't look like she's dumb. Not to me, she don't."

"How are dumb people suppose to look?" I said.

"What I mean is, she looks to me like she's been singin' just like all the rest us been doin'."

"Maybe she's faking it," I said. "Just mouthing the words, doncha know."

He rubbed his chin. "Yeah. That's right, ain't it? That's what she's been doin'. She's just mouthin' the words. How pitiful, the poor little thing. Kinda brings tears to your eyes, don't it? Movin' her lips and nothin' comin' out. Plumb awful."

The man turned around and looked toward the rear of the tent. He seemed anxious. "Wonder where that durn

Pooter done got hisself off to," he said, speaking just above a whisper. "I swear, that boy. He's gonna miss out iffen he don't git hisself here directly."

He took another look behind him. "I bet I know what's done happened. He's done it before, lots of time. He'll wait till after they get done passin' 'round the offerin' plate before he'll come in. He don't do that just at tent revivals. No, sir. He'll do that at church too—every Sunday. His mama, she don't like it none, him doin' thataway."

After we sung the last verse of "Take the Name of Jesus with You," Brother Holcomb spent the next ten- or fifteen-minutes selling men's and women's combs. Along the wider edge of each comb, he said, was a quotation from the *New Testament*.

I found out later the men's comb quoted in part from *1st Corinthians* 11:14—"If a man have long hair, it is shame unto him." The women's comb, on the other hand, quoted part of the next verse —"But if a woman have long hair, it is a glory to her." Brother Holcomb claimed the inscriptions would serve as a daily reminder to males to keep their hair trimmed and to females to keep their hair looking nice.

Someone down front, whom I figured was a plant, yelled out, "But Brother Holcomb, ain't you forgot about them what's baldheaded?"

The congregation broke into laughter. Brother Holcomb, flapping his arms, motioned everyone to quiet down. "What if you were baldheaded, you ask?" He walked over by the piano. "I'm glad you asked. Yes, sir, I'm glad you asked."

He reached into a footlocker and withdrew what looked like a washcloth. He spread it out and held it up so all could see. "I ain't about to leave no baldheaded man out. Not me. No, sir. And you'll find out why come in a minute or two. If there's anybody who respects baldheaded men, it's me." He waved the cloth. "There's scripture on this one here too. It's from *Leviticus* 13:40. Know what it says? It says, *And the man whose hair is fallen off his head, he is bald; yet is he clean.* Other words, it reminds a man who ain't got no hair to wash his head off every now and then—to keep it clean."

That interpretation seemed a stretch to me.

Brother Holcomb approached the edge of the stage, dragging the microphone with him, stand and all. "Now who wants one of these combs or one of these washrags, things what's blessed with Holy Scripture? They ain't but fifty cents each. Why that's about the cost of a 45-RPM record, and you can't comb your hair with no record. Wash it neither.

"And another thing, each comb you buy the money goes to support this ministry. But more importantly, it'll serve as a reminder to take care of your hair and scalp. Each comb and each cloth is also a sacred reminder of this worship experience and the sacrifice at Calvary, and, being such, means it'll serve to bless you time and again. So, come on up here and buy you a blessing. There's only a few of these things left at this price."

Two score or more rushed to the stage to get their combs and washcloths before they all ran out or the price went up. A number of buyers returned to their seats, combing their hair.

With the last purchase rung up, Brother Holcomb drifted back over to the microphone. "All right, friends, we have a special treat for our children and for the young at heart. I wanna introduce to you tonight a young lady who will introduce the newest member of our ministry." He turned and beckoned for Ginger to join him at the microphone. "Come on up here, young lady, and tell the folks who you are."

Ginger bounced to the front as full of pep as a high-school cheerleader at Homecoming. She wore a long skirt and, from where I sat, looked like she no longer wore makeup. "Well, good evening, y'all. I'm Ginger Childree, and boy am I glad to be here tonight with all you wonderful people. I've not heard singing like y'all just did since I was a little girl."

"Excuse me a moment." Ginger turned, ran over to a far end of the stage, and came hurrying back while carrying Kuddles and a vent stand. She positioned the vent stand by the microphone and set Kuddles down, adjusting the long skirt Kuddles now wore.

"Everyone," she continued, "this is Kuddles. You know what? This morning, know what she did? She turned her life over to Jesus. She sure did." Ginger smiled at Kuddles and fiddled with her dress once again. "Will you say something, Kuddles, to all these nice people?"

"Something," Kuddles appeared to say.

"Come on. I mean really," Ginger said, after the laughter died.

Then followed a recounting of the experience Ginger and Kuddles shared earlier in the day. Afterward, came an invitation for all the children to come forward.

As the kids rushed from their seats to join Kuddles and Ginger on stage, the man next to me said, "Why, that woman, she knowed how to talk all along. You can't fool me."

I smiled. "Yeah but look at her. She's making the dummy speak."

The man looked at me like I was nuts. "That dummy, it ain't really the one what's doin' the talkin'. That little woman you see there holdin' it, she's throwin' her voice. That's what's makin' it look like it's talkin'. You didn't know that?"

"Well, I'll be damned," I said, feigning surprise. "I think you're on to something."

"Don't that beat all?" he said, slapping his thigh. "I come here expectin' to see a miracle, somethin' I could tell my grandchilluns I seen. And what do I see? A durn trick, that's what. Wait till I getta hold of Pooter. I betcha he knowed they's gonna try and trick us. No wonder he ain't showed up, durn his sorry hide."

My seatmate was fit to be tied. He stood and pointed to the aisle. "Excuse me, Mister. Lemme slip by you. I believe I can still make it to work, iffen I hurry. I sure am glad I can scoot outta here 'fore they took up the offerin'," he said as he stepped past me.

Ginger and Kuddles engaged for a couple of minutes in some banter, to the delight of the children who sat in a semi-circle before them on the stage. Kuddles seemed to study the children a moment and then appeared to say, "Lemme tell you kids a Bible story. It comes from *Second Kings*, the second chapter, verses 23 and 24. Have any of you children ever heard of the prophet Elisha?"

Two or three children raised their hands, rather hesitantly. I think they lied.

"Well, one day Elisha was walking down this road toward this town, see. And then, all of a sudden like, a bunch of little boys, they come running up and started making fun of Elisha on account of him having a bald head. They were all skipping and shouting, 'Old Elisha's ba-ld! Old Elisha's ba-ld! He ain't got no ha-ir on his he-ad. Old Elisha's ba-ld!'

"Now, boys and girls, was that a nice thing to do—to make fun of some old man because he didn't have no hair on his head?"

"Nooooooo," the children answered as one.

Kuddles' head moved from side to side several times. "No, is right. It certainly wasn't. So, you know what Elisha did? He cursed the little boys. He sure did." There was a pause. "Y'all know what a curse is, don't you?"

The children shook their heads no.

"It's calling down something bad on somebody—asking that something bad happen to him. Old Elisha, he held his arms straight out and wiggled his fingers and said,

I put a curse on all y'all. May a haint or a wicked old witch or something even worse come outta the dark woods yonder and eat each and every one of y'all all up, starting down there with your feet so you'd have to watch it eat you."

The children moaned and made faces.

Kuddles leaned down, her head just above those of the children. "And then, do you know what happened?"

The kids all shook their heads. "Noooooo."

"Why, these two big old mama bears, they come creeping, creeping real, real slow outta the woods, staying in the shadows of the trees, trying real, real hard to keep from being seen. And then . . . and then, those mama bears, they raised themselves up, roared in a mighty voice, and then they *pounced* on those little boys before any of them could get away. And then they killed every last one of those little boys and ate them all up, that's what."

Three or four children screamed, and two of those fled the stage, crying for their mamas who fell over one another in an effort to get to them.

Ginger continued with Kuddles, seemingly unfazed by the commotion. "Why did I tell you this awful story, this scary story? Because that's what can happen when you make fun of somebody who's got something wrong with them, something they can't help. So, the next time you feel like teasing somebody because he wears glasses or is crippled or not smart or something, you stop and you think about what Elisha did to those mean little boys. Because, if you go on and do it, then it might be some bears or maybe something worse than bears will come running after you and, when they catch you, they'll eat you all up or do something else bad to you. Now, the rest of you kids, you go back to your seats and mind how you treat people from now on. Okay?"

The kids took off running.

I stood to take off as well.

A man in the seat to my front turned around to speak to me. His face carried a troubled expression. He said to me, "You reckon that Elisha fella really done that? I mean, did he really have them young'uns killed just because they poked a little fun at him?"

I drew up my shoulders and let them drop. "Well, it's in the Bible, doncha know. Could be a coincidence, I suppose."

After I left the revival meeting, I went by the motel office to check out. I told the desk clerk I'd be leaving the first thing the next morning. When I walked by my truck, I thought I heard the sound of something moving about inside it. I peeped in the window, but I didn't see anything. I tried the back door and the two doors up front. Like when I had checked it earlier, everything seemed nice and tight.

I attributed the sound to my imagination, making me wonder if I had sustained a concussion when Kody's head flew off and knocked me down the steps and those two at my table jumped me.

CHAPTER EIGHT

I got up with the sun the next morning, intending to leave for Abilene as soon as I could load my truck and gas up. Although I still hurt all over, I resolved to continue my journey regardless. I hated not seeing Wally and Ginger one more time, but I'd already said my goodbyes to both.

I removed my suitcase and other things from my room and set them behind my truck to load them in all at once. When I opened the door several minutes later to slide my belongings inside, I got the surprise of my life. There, lying on the floor beside an unopened package of sweet rolls and all curled up in the fetal position, was none other than Dixie St. John.

"What the hell!?" I cried.

Dixie sat up, blinked several times, and took a gander at me through half-closed eyes. "Oh, it's you. Shut the door. Can't you see I'm trying to sleep?" She lay back down.

"What are you doing in my truck, Dixie? And just how'd you get in here? How come you haven't gone back home? Doncha know folks have been worried about you?" I said, talking fast and my voice growing louder with each syllable. Although very angry, at the same time I experienced a measure of relief knowing she had not met with foul play—at least so far as I could tell, she hadn't.

"I'm not gonna tell you again to shut that door," she said, shaking a balled fist at me.

I wasn't about to shut the door. I stepped inside and stood over her. "I asked you some questions, durn your sorry time."

She sat up again. "You don't reckon you could go get me some orange juice, do you?"

Her voice came across so sweet and so soft it took me a little aback. One second, here she was threatening me with physical harm and at the very next she wanted me to do her a favor. Truth to tell, her almost abrupt change of demeanor made me questioned whether Dixie might be on something. But then, I remembered how she could be.

Nonetheless, I stuck to my guns. "I'll get you some, but not until you tell me how you got here and how you got inside my truck."

Dixie yawned. "You gave me the key, don't you remember? Gave it to me back there at that magistrate's office—that store."

I now remembered. I had given her my spare key so she could get into my office and fetch a law book I needed—well, wanted. I really didn't *need* it.

"Uh-huh. But how'd you know where I was?"

"I didn't," she said. "All I knew was you were headed for Shreveport and beyond. I was gonna try to catch up with you, even if that meant traveling all the way to Abilene. The fella I was riding with, he pulled into the service station next door and that's when I just happened to see your truck parked here in front of the motel. I was afraid to ask the desk clerk for your room. In a place like this, I had no idea who might've been in there with you."

"No, whatcha mean is, you were afraid of what he might think you were."

She ignored the slight.

"You been hitch-hiking?" I said. "Is that how you got here?"

"In a way, but not really. Tell you what. I'll fill you in about it later. How about that? But right now, would you please be a sweetheart and go get me some orange juice like I asked you to. I bet that filling station next door has some." She yawned again. "If they don't, just get me some milk."

I cursed myself. I had no choice but to do as Dixie asked; but before I could even walk away, she had yet another request.

"Deloris, have you checked out already?"

"Did it last night."

"You give them the key back yet?"

"No. Why?"

"I'd like to take a shower."

After I returned to my room with Dixie's orange juice and while she showered, I placed a long-distance call to Billy Joe at his home. When he heard my voice, he demanded to know why I was calling him so early. I told him about Dixie. He then lit into me again for leaving her, telling me, if I wanted to live and do well, I'd better not leave her again without my making double sure she was safe.

His threat kinda got under my skin. "Billy Joe," I said, "don't you go to threatening me none. And you know as well as I do Dixie can handle herself. Fact is I'd pity anybody who'd try to tangle with that damn woman."

The other end of the phone grew silent for a moment.

"I'm sorry, Deloris. I didn't mean what I said. You woke me up. I guess I've just been really worried about her, that's all."

"Well, it's not my fault she hadn't tried to call you."

"I know," Billy Joe said. "I know. I'm sorry. Is she all right?"

"Better than I am. I tell you that," I said rubbing my sore shoulder and neck areas.

"I guess she's determined to go to Abilene with you?"

"I'd say so."

Thinking I'd should change the subject now that he'd calmed down, I inquired whether he'd heard anything from the Phillipses. He said he hadn't but went on to point out that today was another day.

After I hung up the telephone, there was a knock at my door. It was the motel manager, a little fella with beaver teeth and pimples.

"Mr. Meek," he said, wringing his hands, "Didn't, uh . . . uh. . . didn't I see . . . uh . . . a woman go into your room . . . uh . . . maybe . . . uh . . . a while ago?"

I looked behind me and then at him again. "I don't know whatcha've seen and whatcha haven't."

"Uh . . . don't I, uh . . . hear the shower running? I believe I do."

"You do?"

"Yes, sir. I, uh . . . I think I do. Uh, tell you what. When, uh . . . she gets all done . . . uh . . . and you, uh, come bring me back the key, that's gonna, uh, cost you, uh . . . another ten bucks. That's what we, uh . . . charge when there's, uh . . . two to the room."

"Since when?"

"Always done it. Don't you remember, I, uh, uh . . . give you and them othern a . . . uh . . . single-occupancy price when, uh . . . uh . . . you come in?"

Dixie hadn't been back in my company no more than thirty minutes and already she'd cost me ten dollars and the price of a carton of orange juice.

I wondered what other costs I'd face on account of her before all was said and done.

* * * * *

We left the motel parking lot and headed for the gas station next door to fill up and have everything checked out before hitting the road for Texas. After telling the station attendant what I wanted done, I looked over at Dixie who busied herself going through all of the romance magazines she'd left in my truck.

"Are they all there?" I asked in a sarcastic voice.

"Lucky you," she snapped back.

"Okay, let's have it."

"Have what?"

"How you got to Shreveport."

"Well, I'll tell you," she said.

She returned her magazines to the spot between the front seats. "After you abandoned me at that bus stop, I knew there was no way for me to ride a bus, not with my bladder acting up and me having to stop so much like I'd been having to do. I know some of the buses—the ones they call the 'Scenicruiser'—I know they've got restrooms on them, but I couldn't see myself using one of those things." She wrapped her arms around herself and shivered.

I laughed to myself, *But you'd use a filthy privy out back of a country filling station, wouldn't you?*

"You'd been gone maybe ten minutes when this route salesman from this bread company came in, toting stuff. You know, loaf bread, hotdog buns—stuff like that. I asked him which way he was going. He told me. I then asked him how far down the road he was going, and he said about another two or three miles and then home. He asked me why I wanted to know. I told him I wanted a ride. He said company policy wouldn't allow that."

She went on to tell me how she managed to talk the bread man into letting her ride with him, explaining to him why she couldn't ride the bus and why she didn't feel like getting out on the highway trying to hitch-hike. The bread man came up with the idea of her being his helper and in that way she wouldn't be considered a hitchhiker but a fellow worker. Dixie jumped at the chance. By the time they worked the last stop, the bread man had invited her to spend the night at his home with him and his wife.

When Dixie met the bread man's wife and told her about her bladder problem being the reason she didn't want to ride the bus, she told Dixie she'd recently suffered from the same condition and offered to help Dixie get an early appointment the next day with her urologist. The doctor attended to Dixie the next morning and wrote her out a prescription.

"I seem much, much better. I don't need to go as often," Dixie said.

Hearing that pleased me to no end. But I still had questions. "Are you telling me the bread man brought you all the way to Shreveport?" I asked.

"No, of course not," Dixie said. "He just set everything in motion. Helped line up things for me. Nice man." She turned her head my way. "Nicer than some people I know."

"Whatcha mean helped line up things for you?"

"Well, he told other route salesmen about my problem. And one by one, they'd pass me off, from one store to the next. You know the bread man'd turn me over to the milk man, who'd turn me over to the cracker man, who'd turn me over to the fella who'd deliver potato chips. Then, I'd ride with the cookie man and next the candy man—all them. Actually, it was kinda fun. They called me 'the package.' " She laughed. "Do I look like a package to you?"

I thought so, but I wasn't about to tell her that.

She laughed again. "You know one thing? I don't think any of the route salesmen ever knew what another one's name was. I rode with two beer salesmen. I hated riding with the soft-drink salesmen. They worked the hardest, having to sort a bunch of dirty bottles and fill up the drink boxes, stack shelves, and all. They smelled the worst too. I guess that's because they sweated the most, doing all they had to do."

"Who brought you to Shreveport?"

"A fuel-tank truck driver. I met up with him somewhere in Bienville Parish. One of the beer salesmen introduced us. It was a good thing too, meeting him. That's how come we happened to stop at the filling station next door. He needed to see to their tanks. While he did that, I thought I'd use the opportunity to go to the restroom and that's when I spotted your stupid truck."

"So, you rode with route salesmen and truck drivers."

"Not always. I rode one time with an insurance man on his debit route for a little while, but that was too slow and sometimes he'd go off the 'beaten path,' so to speak—like when he'd chased down some sharecropper or other poor soul for a dollar or two. I got tired of all that. We parted company at a barbecue joint when we stopped for a bite to eat and I ran into another bread salesman. He was there, delivering some buns and rolls. He'd apparently heard about me."

Dixie paused a moment and then started laughing. "At one point—and you're not gonna believe this, I even rode with a rubber man."

"A rubber man? You mean, like recaps and inner tubes?"

"No, uh-uh. You know, the one who services condom machines at filling stations and so forth."

Dixie stretched out in her seat. "Know what he told me? He said the worst part of his job was having to go into all those dirty toilets, and the second worst was having to count all those quarters from the vending machines. He said I'd really be surprised at the stuff folks wrote on his machines, trying to be funny. You know, graffiti."

I told her it wouldn't surprise me.

"He said he might write him a book one day that collected all those sayings. He said some of them were really hilarious even though they were real dirty, most of them. His favorite was, *For best results, remove foil before use.* I didn't understand that one."

"I bet you didn't," I said.

"What's that suppose to mean?" she said, her voice tinged with indignation.

I didn't answer her. Instead, I asked her what the rubber man looked like.

"Oh, kinda like he'd never, ever need his product."

We sat there a bit, neither one of us saying anything. Then the service attendant knocked on my window. "That'd be eight dollars, Mister."

As I reached for my wallet, he moved his head to the right and then to the left as he peered inside. "That your wife, Sir?"

I handed him a five and three ones. "Why, hell no." Just for laughs, I thought I'd try to get a rise outta Dixie. "Know what this woman done last night? She come and got in my truck—you know, over there at the Polk. So far, it's only cost me ten dollars and a carton of orange juice. And she stayed the whole night too."

The attendant's mouth dropped open. "Really, Mister? Gol…ol…eeebum. Just ten dollars?"

"And don't forget the orange juice," I said with a laugh.

When I pulled away from the pumps and before I could turn into the highway, Dixie slapped me upside the head with a rolled-up romance magazine. "I'll get you back for that."

I rubbed my head. "I was just joking around, Dixie. Anyway, I told the truth."

"That's not anyway to joke about somebody, and you know it. I'm gonna get even with you for that. Don't you worry."

* * * * *

With my head still smarting somewhat from where Dixie had struck me, I drove about twenty minutes before I said another word to her. For her part, she just sat there in her seat reading one of her magazines and acting like nothing in the world had happened. I remembered something Billy Joe told me about her one time. "Deloris," he said, "I think I'd come closer to understanding automatism or radiesthesia than understanding Dixie St. John."

I said, "Billy Joe, I don't know what in the hell you're talking about—automatism or radiesthesia. I don't know what that stuff is."

He said, "See, that's my point."

I guess he was trying to tell me not to even try to figure her out.

As the morning unfolded and the hot sun bore down on us more and more, the inside of my truck started to feel like a sauna. I rolled down my window to let some air blow in. When I did, the wind caught Dixie's hair, making it swirl all about. The wind, to her displeasure, also flipped the pages of her magazine.

She slapped the pages back. "Will you roll that window back up?" she said. "Can't you see I'm trying to read here? The wind's messing up my pages and my hair."

I pulled off onto the shoulder of the road, aiming to let her have it—just like I did the last time I'd stopped to complain about the way she'd been behaving herself. I glared at her. "Dixie, I'm telling you I'm not about to put up with your sass. I'm just not gonna do it. I done left you one time, you know." I rubbed the side of my head. "This still hurts a little, plus I've still got other places that hurt from the other night."

She looked surprised. "What other places? What do you mean the other night?"

I realized she didn't know about the recent unpleasantness at the Bayou Pickin' Parlor, so I told her all about it and what had happened to Wally and me. For the first time since I'd met her, she actually showed me a little compassion—not much, but some.

She leaned over and examined where she'd hit me. "It looks a little red. And that bump there on your forehead, is that where the dummy's head hit you? I hadn't noticed it until now. I'm sorry I hit you as hard as I did, but you shouldn't've said what you did back there. I mean, what if that fella believed you?"

"So, what if he did? Like I told you before, everything I said to him was the truth."

"I don't care if it was. It wasn't so much what you said, but how you said it and where we were right then. It was the implication."

I waved away her complaint. "You've nothing to worry your pretty little head about. You won't never see him again no how."

"You don't know that."

I got back onto the highway and drove a mile or so more before she spoke again. "Since you claim you are in some pain, how about me driving some?"

"You think you can drive this truck?" I said.

The whole time I had known her I had never known or heard of her driving. I figured as pretty as she was she could get any man to haul her fanny anywhere she wanted it to go at any time day or night. Her conning each of those route salesmen into giving her a lift and helping her to catch up with me proved that.

She sighed. "Deloris, how many times have I got to tell you? I can do anything. I'm probably the cleverest soul you've ever met. Now, stop this truck. I'll do the driving for a change."

When I surrendered the wheel to Dixie, I did so with reservations galore.

Just as we entered Texas I heard it; and the moment I heard it a momentary urge to chase after it surged through me, being one, since law school, naturally curious about sirens, if you get my drift. The wail of a siren is music to the ears of a lawyer like me. It equates to trouble, the source of most, if not all, of my and most other lawyers' income. Whether produced by the siren of an ambulance, a fire truck, or a police car, the sound often represents an opportunity for money to be made.

The sound grew closer and closer, louder and louder. I said to Dixie, "Pull over on the shoulder."

"I know to do that. You don't have to tell me," she said as she turned the steering wheel to the right and coasted to a stop alongside the pavement.

The sound continued behind us for a moment and died down.

After a minute or so, a police officer of some sort decked out in a brown and tan uniform and wearing a white cowboy hat came alongside the cab. The officer couldn't have stood much more than a little over four feet tall, and that would've been if he had been wearing elevator shoes. He removed his sunglasses as he peeked inside. His head barely cleared the bottom of the window. "Looka, looka, looka here, I need your license, little lady. Gimme."

"What?" Dixie said, using her normal, intimidating voice. "And just who are you, of all people, calling somebody 'little,' you pip-squeak?"

Her response made me groan. I knew from the experience I'd had in representing traffic offenders by the bag full that you didn't talk to an officer of the law that way. A smart mouth usually voids any discretion an officer may have regarding whether to ticket a suspected traffic offender or not.

The officer backed up a bit. "I'm talking to you, that's who."

Dixie's attitude changed in an instant. I figured it'd dawned on her that she should've been nicer to him. He may have been a pip-squeak all right, but that star on his chest not only made him a whole lot taller but a hellava lot more important. She batted her eyes at him. "Oh, did I do something wrong, sweetie? You're a cute little thing. You know that?"

The officer frowned. "Gimme your driver's license right now, else I'll show you what us cute little pip-squeaks can do."

Dixie turned my way, her eyebrows knitted together all of a sudden. Something about the way in which she looked at me told me to prepare myself for the worse.

"Officer," Dixie said, in a voice sweeter than a bonbon, "I'm sorry, but I don't have one with me right now."

I decided to intervene. "Officer, this is my truck. I decided to let her drive some since there wasn't much traffic. Plus, I was kinda in an accident recently and haven't fully recovered from it and still hurt a little."

The officer bit his lip before stepping closer to the truck. "So, this here thing, this truck, it belongs to you—Deloris Meek, is it?"

"One in the same," I said with a touch of pride in my voice.

"Deloris, huh? Could I say something? Ain't that a girl's name?"

"Don't think so. Since I'm a boy and that's my name, that makes it a boy name, doesn't it?" I said with a laugh.

"I don't know 'bout that," he said, without cracking a smile. "You got a driver's license, Deloris?"

I withdrew my wallet from my back pocket and flipped it open. "Yes, sir. See here."

I hated saying "sir" to the officer. He appeared much younger than me. And I didn't like his acting so familiar with me, calling me by my Christian name.

"All right," he said, "this is what we're all gonna do. Looka, looka, looka here. Y'all are gonna switch seats, and, Deloris, I want you to follow me. Got that?"

"And just where is it we're going, Officer?" I said. "Mind telling me?"

"Justice of the Peace. Yeah, yeah, yeah."

"For what?"

"Well, she ain't got no driver's license. That's number one. Number two, for suspicion."

"Suspicion?" I said. "Suspicion of what?"

"Prostitution. And I'm hitting you with aiding and abetting prostitution. Yeah, yeah, yeah. How's that grab you?"

"Say what?" both Dixie and I yelled.

"Y'all heard me." The officer put a hand on his revolver, a weapon almost as big as he was. "Now do what I done told you, and then y'all wait for me to come around. Yeah, yeah. And stay close behind."

He pointed his finger at us. "Looka, looka, looka here. If y'all get the bright idea to try and run from me, I'll shoot out them tires you got—all of them. And don't think I can't do it neither." He withdrew a revolver from its holster and blew once on the gun barrel. "Catch on? And if that don't do the trick, then I know what will. Now, y'all change seats while I go get my vehicle. It ain't gonna take me but a couple of seconds. Hear what I say?"

About the time I got situated behind the wheel, the officer drove around and honked his horn, as if we didn't recognize him. He motioned for me to follow as he pulled forward.

CHAPTER NINE

We drove until we came upon a cement block building with a sign over the front door that read, "The Honorable Travis Crockett Monroe, Justice of the Peace." I wondered why his name didn't include that other hero of the Alamo, Jim Bowie.

The officer pulled into one of the parking spaces out front and motioned for me to park on the north side, next to the building. Dixie and I exited the truck and met him at the door.

The faint sound of harmonica music wafted to my ears from inside the building. "Is that what I think it is, Officer?" I said. "Is that somebody playing 'Nobody Knows the Trouble I've Seen'?"

The officer cupped a hand to his ear. "Oh, that's just the justice. He's fixing to hear a case. He does that sometime just before he gets started. Says it relaxes him."

"Relaxes him?"

"What he says."

"How about the defendants? Relax them?"

The officer chuckled. "Oh, the justice, he don't care none about them. Yeah, yeah, yeah."

I found that little bit of information somewhat discouraging. I gathered the justice had a strange sense of humor and even stranger sense of fairness and decorum.

The music stopped the moment we opened the outside door. Once inside, I discovered the building contained only one room, its walls paneled with dark wood and its floor overlaid with a black tile. Because closed venetian blinds blocked out the sun, it took a moment for my eyes to adjust to the reduced lighting. A droning window air-conditioner, aided by the semi-darkness, gave the room a slight chill. The room exuded doom in every nook and corner.

Toward the back of the room and behind a beat-up mahogany desk sat a man with long white hair, light-colored eyes, and sunken cheeks. His long legs, crossed at the ankles, rested atop the desk. He wore a white cowboy shirt, a tan cowboy hat, dungarees, and a pair of scuffed-up, brown cowboy boots. The man's skin had an unnatural paleness about it, so much so I would have figured him for a corpse except for the rise and fall of his chest as he breathed. I guessed him to be about seventy to seventy-five years old. Behind him stood unfurled flags of the State of Texas and of the Confederacy and between them framed portraits of Sam Houston and Robert E. Lee. On the far side of the Texas flag was a sign that read, "Don't even ask." It didn't explain what not to ask for.

The officer swept his arm toward a line of several high-back, cane-bottom chairs on the left side of the room. An equal number of chairs lined the opposite wall. The officer tilted his head at Dixie and me, and we both sat down on the left side. He remained by the door, his arms folded and trying his dead level best to look badass.

A tall, middle-age man with a ruddy complexion and dressed in paint-spattered, faded blue overalls stood in front of the justice's desk, alternately twisting a beat-up painter's hat and scratching a ring of gray hair around his otherwise bald head. As near as I could make out, based on the justice's opening remarks, the man's wife had earlier obtained a warrant for his arrest.

The justice unfolded a long, blue sheet of paper. "You Fayrow Coggins?"

"Yeah, uh huh . . . I mean, yessir."

"Have I gotcha name right? Is it really Fayrow? F-a-y-r-o-w?"

"Yessir, that's right. Fayrow. Midwife, she kinda went off the beam and got the spelling all messed up. She wasn't no speller, iffen you know what I mean. 'Posed be like in the Bible. You know, P-h-a-r-a-o-h. Pharaoh. My brother, Mama named him 'Prince.' And my sister, she goes by 'Queen Ester.' We call her 'Queenie' for short. You had her up here a time or two. You know, for a'sellin' jar whiskey. She's got a no-count husband and has to sell—"

The justice raised a hand to cut Fayrow off. "Gotcha." After peering at the document close up for a moment, he slapped it. "This here don't look good, Fayrow." He shook his head. "Not good at all. Not to me, it don't."

"Say it don't?"

"No, it don't."

Justice Monroe removed his feet from the desk and dropped them to the floor. "I'm fixing to read you what that wife of yours says you done." He again held the paper up close to his eyes. "First thing she says is you talked real mean and hateful to her and, while you were doing it, your voice got so loud both the dog and the cat, they high-tailed it outta the kitchen. She says she ain't seen them since."

"She say that, sir?" Fayrow said. "We ain't even got no dog. Ain't got no cat neither."

"Don't interrupt me. I ain't through telling you all she's said here. There's some other things. She says she told you she was sick with the high blood and felt sick as a dog. You then told her you didn't care if she up and died and anyway you were gonna send her on back to her mama so she could take care of her, that you had better things to do than to look after an old hag like her. Then, she says, you made her go pack up her things and go sit in the truck. You later drove her to town to catch a bus. She says you left her there all by herself, with her begging you not to do it, and her feeling dizzy and sick on her stomach. Says she felt like she was gonna puke."

I leaned over to whisper something to Dixie, but before I could finish what I wanted to tell her she told me to shush, that she was interested in what the justice was telling the man.

The justice continued with the accusation. "Anyway, your wife, she says she didn't catch the bus but went and spent the night with the woman what cooks at the café just across the street from the bus stop. The next morning the cook, she come and took her to see Doctor Billy Seaborn, and he give her some pills to help her with the high blood. A day later, the cook brought her on back to where y'all been staying at and when you come home that evening you started in on her again. She says the whole time all that was going on you had you a big old butcher knife in your hand."

"It wasn't no butcher knife, Judge, Your Honor, sir. It was one of them little ol' pear knives. I was a'peelin' me a pear right then. I was hungry, and she ain't fixed me not one blessed thing to eat. Not no nothin'."

"Well, I don't know about all that, Fayrow," the justice responded. "She says you had a butcher knife. She claims you said all kinda ugly things about her, calling her names and so forth. Says you were carrying on something awful. And what you said and the way you were acting, it scared her pretty good, especially cause you had you a knife in your hand. That's why she come here and took out a warrant on you."

"Lemme ask you, Judge, Your Honor, sir." Fayrow leaned forward. "Just cause she told you all that stuff, that don't make it so, now do it?"

"Well, for right now it does," the justice responded.

"It do?" Fayrow dropped his head. "Well, I ain't mean to scare her none by a'peelin' me no pear. But I do wanna be shed of her. I ain't gonna lie about that none. I say let her head on back to them what raised her. Them's the ones what made her like she is. Let them put up with her sass and her old bossy ways—hatefulest woman the Lord ever made, she sure is. She lay 'round just 'bout all the time, a'readin' all them ol' trashy magazines of hern, a'primpin' and a'complainin' and everything—a'tellin' me how sorry I am and how my family, it ain't no count either.

"I work twelve, thirteen hours most days, and I come home and there'll be dust on just everything but the knobs to the TV. Floor, it ain't be swept since that tornado blowed through here last year and sucked my roof clean off, a'takin' the floor with it. She don't appreciate nothing I do for her. For her birthday, I give her a brand new reconditioned vacuum cleaner. And you know what? The cord to it, it's still all quarreled up like it was when I bought it. That's the Lord's truth.

"I tell you, Judge, Your Honor, sir, I'm sick and tired of it, so much so I don't care iffen you put me under the jail. Least there, it'll be peace and quiet—uh-huh—and I won't have to listen to her bellyachin' no more—you know what I'm a'sayin'? Iffen it means a'choosin' twixt jail and a'livin' with that hellcat, I hope the judge, he gives me a hundred years—a thousand even."

The justice lit a cigarette and bent forward. "So, I take it, Fayrow, you admit everything your wife sets forth in this here warrant, except for the knife. That right?"

Fayrow's chest swelled. "Iffen it gits me away from that woman, yes, sir, I sure nuff do. But like I done told you while ago, just cause she said it, that don't make it so."

The justice scribbled something on the warrant. "All right, then. I'm gonna have to bump your case on over to the county judge. I'll let them deal with it over yonder. Sounds like this might could be an assault."

"Yes, sir. That's all right with me. Just sail it on over. Iffen you want me to, I'll even run it over there for you my own self. Me, I'm tired of all this here stuff."

"Yeah. Well, okay. Now, take a seat over there next to the wall. I've got me another matter to deal with. When I'm through with it, I'll get Runt to drive you to the jail. I'll do my best to get you there in time for you to get you something to eat. Okay?"

The justice looked around at the officer and raised his hand, opening and closing his fingers. "All right, Runt, let's have it. Whatcha got here, a speeder?"

Runt looked our way and motioned for us to join him in front of the justice's desk.

As we went forward, the justice reached for his harmonica and slipped it into his shirt pocket. That action disappointed me. I had hoped he play a little tune before our case as he had done before Fayrow's and provide Dixie and me with some clue about how he might deal with us.

"Speeder?" Runt said. "Better than that, Your Honor. These two say they are Dixie St. John and Deloris Meek. They're from outta state. I caught the woman driving without a license. Yeah, yeah, yeah."

The justice, frowning, shook his head. "When will they ever learn?"

"I dunno, sir. Never, I don't reckon," Runt said, his tone one of commiseration.

The justice glanced first at me and then at Dixie. He kept his eyes on Dixie for obvious reasons. "Answer me this, Runt. Which'un is Deloris and which'un is Dixie?"

"Excuse me, Your Honor." The officer put his hand on my shoulder. "This'un here is Deloris."

The judge studied me a second or two and repeated my given name. "You sure about that, Runt? 'Deloris,' ain't it a girl's name? And 'Dixie,' I seem to recall a ballplayer with that name. Dixie Howell, maybe?"

I started to say something, but before I could Runt answered for me. "Can I tell you something? I was all for his name being a girl's name too, but he says no it ain't one because he's a boy and that's his given name. But I can't see why that should make no never mind. Girl's names are for girls and ain't for them what's got a different kind of plumbing. I mean, would you name a girl Dexter or

Clarence? No, you wouldn't. They're made different down there, and that's what makes a girl's name a girl's name and a boy's name a boy's name."

"Yeah, you make a good point," the justice muttered. He nodded toward Dixie. "Mind how you talk, though. There's a lady present. But I think I get what you're saying. What you mean is, calling a bull Betsy, that don't make it a cow."

"Exactly," Runt allowed.

The justice shifted around in his chair. "Say you got more'n just speeding, Runt?"

Runt smiled. "Yeah, yeah, yeah. Sure do. I'm gonna show you this woman here, she ain't no lady. Not by no long shot."

"She ain't?" The justice's voice had the ring of disappointment.

"No, sir, she ain't. Your Honor, I've got a first cousin, twice removed, who works at this gas station near Shreveport. You met him once—Virgil Pickett, Jr. His mama was a Crawford. Anyway, before I left to go on duty this morning, Mama, she asked me would I mind taking him some of her fig preserves and some jars of some other things she'd made to give to his mama whenever he got off work. He works the late-night shift there—from one to eight in the morning, thereabouts. I told her no, I didn't mind taking it to him at all.

"So, when I seen him, he told me I should be on the lookout for a lawyer fella in a milk truck what wasn't a milk truck no more. He said the lawyer was traveling with a woman pretty as the Queen of Sheba. He felt like, cause they turned left, they might be headed for Texas, but he couldn't swear to it. He said when he went to ask for the gas money the lawyer fella told him the woman was a ten-dollar whore he'd picked her up at the motel next door. It's the one what's called the Polk Inn. It ain't no secret whores work that place morning, noon, and night. Does a big lunchtime business, too, and they don't even have no café there. Yeah, yeah, yeah."

The justice leaned far back in his chair and looked up toward the ceiling, rubbing his chin. "Hmmmm. So, Runt, I'm guessing you're thinking prostitution and aiding and abetting prostitution. That right?"

Runt's chest swelled, and he smiled so big you'd thought he'd arrested Bonnie and Clyde. "Yeah, yeah, yeah. That's exactly what I was thinking. I done good, didn't I, Judge? You know, catching them like I done before they could get started good with their devilment by breaking the best laws in the whole wide world." His chest swelled. "The laws of the Republic of Texas."

The justice flipped forward and adjusted his cowboy hat. "Okay, Dixie, Dixie St. John. That name kinda sounds fake to me. You know, like 'Mary Smith' or 'Jane Brown.' That fella with you, he your pimp, I'm guessing?"

Dixie took my measure. "My pimp? You gotta be kidding me. Him? No way."

Justice Monroe put a tongue to his cheek. "Okay, then, whatcha gotta say for yourself, Dixie, if that really is your name?"

"Judge, Justice—which?"

"Either one. Suit your fancy."

"Judge, I want you to take a good, long look at me. Now, do I look like a prostitute to you? Do I? I mean, really?" Dixie stood straight, unsmiling, her arms to the side, staring straight ahead.

Justice Monroe did as Dixie asked him to do. He took a look—a good, long one. "Nope," he said, "I can't say you do—least like none I ever seen before."

"And that's because I'm not one. I work for Billy Joe Pratt, attorney at law. I'm traveling with Deloris Meek, who's also a lawyer but he's not as good a one as Lawyer Pratt is. Lawyer Pratt's the best."

Dixie knew how to hurt me.

"Anyhow, when I found out Deloris was headed to Abilene to look for a lost heiress, I decided I wanted to go along with him because I've never been to Texas before. I had some vacation time coming. Then too, I figured I might be of some help to him, being I was a legal secretary and know a little something about the law practice and all—probably more than he does, if the truth be known."

The justice smiled and winked at Runt.

"So, I took some of my vacation time to do it—to travel with him. But—and I'll have to be honest—he didn't seem to appreciate my wanting to help him, or even my help when I gave it. Why, I even helped him win a case the other day before we left our home state. The man was charged with indecent exposure. It was pretty much me who got him off, though I kinda feel bad about it. But that's another story.

"When we got to Mississippi, he picked up these two hitchhikers—a man and this silly little woman. They were show-biz types, if you catch my drift. I wouldn't have picked them up myself, but Mr. Know-it-all here, he stopped and took them aboard, not knowing the first thing about them. I advised him not to do it, but he went right on ahead and did it. Didn't listen to me. I don't know why, although I got my own ideas." Dixie turned my way and smirked. "You know what happened after that? A little while later, him and the hitchhikers, they drove off and left me after we stopped for gas and I'd gone to use the ladies' room. Can you believe that?"

The justice laid an angry look on me. "He done that? A pretty girl like you? Drove off and left you? Whereabouts was this?"

I couldn't believe what Dixie was doing. I raised my hand. "Judge, could I say something, please sir?"

"You'll get your chance when I'm ready to give it to you, bub. Now shut up," the justice barked. He motioned for Dixie to continue.

"You asked me where he ran off and left me at? We were still in Mississippi, where I'd never been in my whole life. Another thing I was about to tell you, I was sick too. I was having bladder trouble. I was having to go every thirty minutes, it seemed like. But that didn't seem to matter to Deloris Meek. No, he viewed it as something that was inconveniencing him. Also, he'd begun talking hateful and disrespectful to me.

"Fortunately for me, after they went and left me high and dry—him and his brand-new friends—I met this real kind, sweet woman. She was the wife of a route salesman I met where we'd stopped at and was nice to me. She took me in and helped me get to a doctor to see about me. Later on, she and her husband, they arranged for my transportation so I could catch up with Deloris and his buddies and give them each one a piece of my mind for leaving me like they did, and me sick as a dog."

"Where was it you caught up with him at, pretty lady? Shreveport, I'm guessing?"

Dixie sniffled and wiped the side of one eye. "Yes, sir. Shreveport, there at some cheap motel called the Polk Inn."

"I know the place," the justice blurted out. His face suddenly took on a red hue. "What I mean to say is, I've heard tell of it."

Dixie turned toward me and gave me a steady look for a few seconds before continuing. "And the silly little woman? Why, she wasn't anywhere to be seen. I learned the man she was with when Deloris picked them both up out in the middle of nowhere, he was squirreled away in his motel room. I found out later him and Deloris there, they'd been in some kinda fight at a honky-tonk. Both of them'd been beat up pretty good. No telling what they'd been up to for that to've happened. Found out, too, the little woman had taken up with a tent preacher. A tent preacher. Don't that beat all? Shows you what kinda person she was, going from one man to another. Passed from one man to another, like she was an offering plate. Disgusting."

The justice shifted some papers about on his desk. "What about him telling that fella at the gas station you weren't nothing yourself but a ten-dollar whore?"

"I could've killed him for saying that. I don't know why he did it, and me a private secretary to Billy Joe Pratt, a famous trial lawyer. I suppose he did it to hurt me further. I let him have it for saying that, though. Ask him about that, why don't you? He'll tell you." Dixie paused. "That's my story, Your Honor. I plead for your mercy and kindness, the sort of mercy and kindness that Texas is famous for. One more thing, and I'll shut up. If you need Lawyer Pratt's telephone number to verify my employment with him, I've got it right here in my purse."

The justice stared at Dixie for a moment, his lips puckered so they reminded me of a horse collar. Then he smiled. "Well, what we have here is hearsay evidence that you're a ten-dollar whore. Here's my ruling. If you are a whore—and I ain't saying you are one—all I'm saying is if you are a whore—you sure as hell ain't no ten-dollar one. Bottom line is the court ain't gonna issue no prostitution warrant against you."

Dixie beamed. "Thank you, Your Honor, for seeing the truth. You are a very wise man. We need more like you serving as judges. I wish we had you for a judge where I come from. It'd be a lot better place."

Justice Monroe stared at me, his eyes boring into me like a power drill. "All right, lawyer man, I'll hear from you—although I don't know why. You ain't gonna do nothing but lie noways. I can tell by looking at you. But before you get started on that, weren't you sitting right there when I questioned Fayrow yonder a while ago? You heard all that, didn't you?"

I responded first with a nod, followed by a "Yes, sir."

"Sounds kinda like you and him done just about the same thing, don't it?"

I shook my head. "I don't think so, Judge."

"Yeah? Well, his wife was sick, and this pretty lady was sick. You run off and left her somewheres, just like he went and done. You talked bad to her. You getting the picture now? Sounds to me like you committed abuse of some kind. Assault maybe, plus common-law jeopardation under color of law, I'm thinking."

"Common-law jeopardation? I've never heard of such a—"

"That's right," the judge snapped. "Common-law jeopardation, and under color of law too, don't forget. I mean, y'all each one run off, leaving a helpless woman all by her lonesome. That's putting somebody in jeopardy right there. You don't need no law degree to know that. You can't go around giving somebody the heave-ho whenever you feel like it, especially where they ain't never been before, like you done."

The justice went on. "Why, she might've been killed or robbed or beat up. I don't know what all might've happened to her, and you don't neither." He paused. "Course, now, you ain't had no butcher knife in your hands like Fayrow there—least not one, I heard about. But you probably had you a pocket knife on you, didn't—"

Fayrow interrupted. "Judge, like I say, I had me a pear knife—not no butcher knife. I was a'peelin' me a pear."

Justice Monroe turned and stared at Fayrow. "You keep quiet. I don't wanna hear another peep outta you. Got that? You keep on, and I'll hit you with a contempt."

Fayrow hung his head and muttered a yes, sir.

"Can I say one more thing, Judge?" I asked.

"I reckon so."

"Okay. Let's just say everything you just said is the truth—"

"You calling me a liar, fella?" He stood and waved at the officer who scrambled over to the judge's side and glared at me.

"No, sir. It's just a hypothetical."

"A hypo what?"

"A hypothetical question. Just for argument sake, you might say. If the facts really are as she told them, they all happened in Mississippi and Louisiana, right?"

"Right."

"Well," I said, "you don't have any kind of jurisdiction over anything that might've happened outside of Texas, now do you? You know, like in Mississippi or Louisiana."

The justice considered what I asked him, looking this way and that. All of a sudden, he yanked off his hat and sailed it across the room where it landed at Faryrow's feet "Dadgummit. Now look whatcha done made me do."

He turned to Fayrow "Lemme have that back." Fayrow picked up the hat and sailed it over to the justice.

"You durn lawyers," the justice said, stuffing his hat back upon his head, "y'all are gonna be the ruination of this country, what with all your shenanigans and all your tricks and whatnot. You're one clever devil, ain't you? But I gotta enforce the law, even when it's stupid."

His face had turned the color of Georgia clay. "Okay. You're right. I didn't think about that 'juris fiction' crap or whatever it's called. Durn it all." He gestured at me. "So, get your sorry behind on outta here. You're free to go. I can't do nothing about what happened in Mississippi or Louisiana. Wished I could, but I can't. So, get the heck outta my sight. I hate you even coming to Texas. We don't need your kind here. No, sir, we don't."

"Justice?" Runt said, "What about that driving without a license charge?"

"What about it? Did she say she didn't have one?"

"My best recollection is she said she didn't have none with her. Yeah, yeah, yeah."

"Boy, listen to me. Not having a license and not having a license *with you*, them's two different things. Case dismissed." Justice Monroe smiled at Dixie. "Take care, little lady, and drive carefully. If you have any more trouble outta that fella, you call me and durn if I won't jail his big butt, even if I have to look for something in the U.N. Charter or the Book of Church Order of the Presbyterian Church in the United States to hang my hat on."

Dixie and I turned to walk out when Fayrow piped up. "Judge, Your Honor, sir, could I please ask you somethin' other?"

"What?"

"Reckon long as you a'lettin' folks go, how 'bout me, sir?"

The justice grumped and folded his arms tight against his chest. "Oh, why the hell not? If the law won't allow me to hold him, damn if I'm gonna let it hold you neither. Get on outta here before I change my mind," he said, waving Fayrow away as he had done me and reaching for his harmonica.

When we reached the truck, Dixie and I stood for a few seconds watching Fayrow make tracks. As he disappeared over a small hill, Dixie said to me, "From now on, mind the things you say to me or about me. I promised you this morning I'd get even with you, and I did. Now we're even."

"But Dixie, that old fool came close to locking me up."

"Oh, I figured you'd come up with something clever and get yourself off. I didn't worry about that one second."

"But what if I hadn't, then what?"

Dixie smiled. "I don't answer hypothetical questions, now that I know what one is."

CHAPTER TEN

I decided to do all the driving after the unpleasant encounter with the police officer and our appearance before the justice of the peace. Actually, Dixie's lack of a driver's license made that decision for me. I took it rather slow, stopping several times for this or that reason but mainly for the purpose of simply walking around and stretching. I had begun to experience considerable discomfort in my lower back. At first, I attributed it to my sitting for so long a time behind the wheel as I drove or to the blows I took from Olive and Grover there at the Bayou Pickin' Parlor. But the ache soon grew into pain, a pain that seemed to become more intense with each passing minute. I tried treating it with some buffered aspirin, but that didn't help at all.

We got to Weatherford, Texas sometime before 4:00 p.m. I wheeled into the parking lot of the first filling station I came to and killed the engine. The pain had now reached a point that I could barely concentrate on driving.

"What's the matter?" Dixie asked. She actually sounded concerned. And well she should have been, as much as I hurt.

I pushed my hand against the left side of my lower back. "I've got the worse pain of my life. I really think I need to see a doctor or a chiropractor, one. I've pulled something, I think. Hurts like the dickens."

"My goodness," Dixie said, giving me a worried look. "Stay put while I go inside and ask them where one is. Back in a jiffy."

Dixie scrambled out of the truck and dashed inside. She returned in minutes with written directions to a medical clinic.

Once there, I got almost immediate attention. A nurse attended me first and expressed the opinion that I might have a kidney stone. A physician—a urologist named Doctor Isadore Cohen—saw me about thirty or forty minutes later, although it seemed like hours. The doctor, a soft-spoken young man with a distinct Texas accent, ordered an X-ray. It confirmed his suspicions. He called what I had a "renal calculus," a fancy word for a kidney stone. He ordered me hospitalized.

"Tell you what, Mr. Meek," Doctor Cohen said, standing over me as I lay on the examination table, "I'm prescribing a powerful painkiller for you and getting you admitted to the hospital. What I want you to do is, each time you urinate I want you to strain your urine and let's see if you've passed the stone. From the picture we got, it's a size you should be able to pass easily enough. For the time being, let's just engage in some 'watchful waiting.' If the stone doesn't pass within a day or so, then we might try something else."

"Something else? You mean surgery?"

"Let's don't talk about surgery right now. Just something else, okay? So, drink lots of water and strain your urine for me. They'll get you a strainer at the hospital and bring to you. Let them know now, if you pass it. In fact, save it for us to look at." He patted me on the shoulder and smiled at me. "Any questions?"

The hospital admitted me right away and assigned me to a double room. Dixie, her high heels clicking, followed close behind the orderly who rolled me in a wheelchair down a short hallway and up one floor on an elevator. I lost count of the number of things he bumped into, so busy he was turning around to ogle Dixie.

When we entered the room, I noticed a drawn curtain separated my area from the one next to the window. As I rounded the foot of my bed, I noticed I had a roommate, a young man, in his early twenties I'd say. He sat in a chair by the window, his right shoulder all bandaged up. I spoke to him when our eyes met, but he only nodded at me.

I hated having to share a room with a perfect stranger. I remember the story Billy Joe told me about his having to do that one time and how uncomfortable that made him feel, especially when the other man's mama came to visit, bringing with her a ton of other folks. Billy Joe said they all stood around, praising the Lord, praying, and singing gospel songs for at least an hour. I asked him whether they sung *a cappella*, and he said, "Hell no. One of them'd brought a damn banjo."

I hoped mine wouldn't have any visitors, particularly the singing kind. It was bad enough having him in the same room with me, let alone having to let a bunch of other strangers come traipsing in and gaping at me like I was some kinda caged animal at the zoo. Besides, the room they'd placed me in was rather small and not suited for a lot of company, furnished as it was with only two beds, two nightstands, and two chairs. It had no telephone.

I also had another complaint. A faint odor of disinfectant hung about the room like unwanted in-laws. I speculated the hospital spread the stuff around for two reasons: one, to goad patients into getting well faster; and two, to coax visitors into either limiting their stay or keeping away entirely.

Dixie noticed the odor right off. She wrinkled her nose almost the second we entered the room. "What's that smell? I don't think I can put up with that. I'm glad it's you and not me that's got to stay here tonight."

"Thanks a lot, Dixie," I grumbled as the orderly helped me onto the bed. "You can leave anytime you feel like it, doncha know. I don't need you here. In fact, you can head on back home for all I care, especially after that trick you pulled this morning in court."

"Tell you what," she said from the foot of my bed, "while you get yourself all comfy, I'll go down and get your suitcase so you can change into your pajamas. Which one they in?"

"The small one."

"Want me to get them out for you?"

"You can. They're the Donald Duck ones."

"Donald Duck?"

"Donald Duck."

"O . . . kay," she said, making a face.

"Mama gave them to me, if you must know. They were supposed to be a joke."

"Well, if so, it keeps getting funnier—a big old man like you wearing Donald Duck jammies in a hospital." She shook her head. "I bet after they discharge you, they'll talk about it for years around here."

Dixie headed out, the orderly rushing to follow her. No sooner had she closed the door than my roommate started up. "I'm so pitiful," he whined. "Don't nobody care I got myself shot, and I tell the doc my shoulder still hurts something awful, but he don't act like he even hears me. Oh, me. Oh, me."

My eyes grew heavy—the effect, I suppose, of the tablets Doctor Cohen had given me before I left for the hospital. In fact, I drifted right off to sleep.

* * * * *

I don't know how long I slept. When I awoke the room seemed somewhat darker and occupied only by my roommate and me. He must've heard me moving about because he started going on again about how pitiful he was and how nobody cared about his getting shot. I sure as heck didn't, the way he kept complaining. It almost got to the point where I wished they'd aimed for a spot right between his durn eyes.

I still wore my regular clothes, but minus the shoes. My pajamas sat on top of my bedside table next to a urinal and a kitchen strainer. I still had pain in my lower back, but it didn't hurt as badly as before.

Feeling the urge to pee, I set up on the side of the bed, reached for the strainer, positioned it over the urinal, and let go. About mid-stream, who just happened to waltz in? Dixie St. John, that's who.

"Oh, sorry," she said with a laugh. "Look at you. Always poking fun at something."

Her barging in like she did caused an interruption of things, and I quickly turned away from her. "Didn't anybody ever teach you to knock before going into somebody's room? I swear to goodness, Dixie."

The only answer I got were the sounds of a door easing shut and of a woman laughing so hard I feared she might go into convulsions. Her laughter embarrassed me because I didn't know exactly what she was laughing at—the sight of my activity at the moment or the primary tool that allowed me to engage in it.

I finished the process and examined the strainer—nothing there but disappointment.

A minute or so later, someone knocked on the door and spoke in a high-pitched, child-like voice. "Mr. Meek, may I please come in, pretty please?"

Of course, it was Dixie, doing a poor job of disguising her voice.

She stole into the room, gritting her teeth. "Spotted anything yet?" she whispered.

I dropped back onto the bed. "No, durn it all. And I still hurt, but not like I did."

"Bless your little heart," Dixie said, using baby talk. "Somebody once told me the pain you get with a kidney attack is worse than when a woman's in labor."

"I wouldn't know. I just know it's bad. And besides, I haven't gotten completely over the beating I got the other night."

* * * * *

I think I must've dozed off again because I awoke when I heard Dixie speak to someone just outside my room. "Evening, ma'am. And how are you?" she said.

"Thankful, praise the Lord," came a quivering voice. "If you don't mind, missy, I'd like to step in there to see about those two fellas."

I heard the door open and some footsteps. I pretended to be asleep.

"And why are you here, ma'am?" Dixie said from the foot of my bed. "You with the hospital?"

"Oh, no, darling. I'm with the Living for Jesus Friendship Church out in the county. Name's Ora Jean Pickens, but most folks, they just call me Sister Ora. Jesus—Bless his precious name—He wants us Christians to visit folks who're having a hard time. So, while I do the sick and the shut-in, other folks from my church, they do the shut-out and the shut-up. The preacher, he does the shut-down."

"The shut-down?"

"Yessum. You know, them what's dead."

"I see."

I opened my eyes a little ways to get a peep at my visitor. A tiny woman, she wore a plain, black dress and had what my mama would call a dowager's hump. Sister Ora brought an odor into the room that reminded me of wet socks or mold or something I couldn't quite make out, and it was strong enough to overcome the disinfectant. A red lipstick smeared on her huge lips as well as a beyond the two edges of her mouth gave her the look of a happy clown. The amount of rouge she had applied to her cheeks would have made an undertaker proud. In the crook of one arm, she cradled a large, well-worn purse linked to a strap hung from the shoulder. Part of a book that had a black cover and golden leaves stuck out from the purse.

"You and him, y'all not from around here, I'm thinking."

"No," Dixie said.

"Has the doctor told you yet what's wrong with your husband?"

Dixie laughed. "He's not my husband. Not by a long shot."

"He's not?"

"Heavens to Betsy, no."

"And who's your doctor, if you don't mind me asking?"

"His doctor, you mean? I think his name is Cohen."

Sister Ora smiled sweetly. "That'd be Doctor Izzy—Doctor Isadore Cohen. Wonderful doctor, especially for somebody who's got an old cannnnn … cer," she said in almost a whisper.

That disclosure shocked me, causing me to take a deep breath and open my eyes. Neither Dixie nor Sister Ora seemed to notice my reaction, however, since they kept right on discussing my situation.

"Oh, but Deloris doesn't have cancer," Dixie said. "Just a kidney stone."

I saw Sister Ora bring both hands to her mouth and heard her take a deep breath. "Is that what Doctor Izzy told y'all? Oh, my," she said removing her hands.

"Way I understood it," Dixie said.

"Uh-huh. Okay, then, if that's what he says."

I regarded her tone as holding a measure of disbelief about the doctor's diagnosis.

A few seconds later Sister Ora whispered to Dixie, but loud enough for me to hear, "You think he's asleep?"

I shut fast my eyes.

"I would think so," Dixie said. "They've given him a bunch of pain pills and such."

Sister Ora continued to whisper. "Just between us, I think your boyfriend—"

"He's not my boyfriend."

"Your boss man, then."

"He's not my boss man either."
"Brother?"
"No."
"Not your daddy?"
"No. We're not kin. He's just somebody I happen to be with at the moment."
"Just somebody you happened to be with, you say?"
"Right."
"At the moment?"
"Yes."
"I see. Least, I think I do."

I heard who I think was the old woman take a deep breath and exhale.

"Well anyway," she said after a short pause, "as I was fixing to tell you, I think he's got an old cannnn . . . cer. They don't call Doctor Izzy in on somebody when all's he got is just a little old kidney stone. No, he's got an old cannnn . . . cer, all right. I mean, to have Doctor Izzy for his doctor, he's just gotta have one. What it is, they just haven't gotten around to telling him the bad news yet. But they will. They'll tell him directly. They won't keep it from him, not for long. They'll tell him in time for him to get right with the Lord."

I didn't know whether to believe the old woman or not. I preferred not to, though no doubt about it she was definitely making me nervous. For one thing, I couldn't imagine my doctor not leveling with me about my condition, even if I was a stranger to him. I continued to act like I was asleep, though I opened my eyes just a wee, wee bit.

Sister Ora shook her head slowly and made a sad face. "Look at your friend, laying there. Poor thing. He doesn't have the slightest idea he's not long for this old world of ours. An old kidney cannnn . . . cer, it's a bad one. I hope he's saved. Do you know if he's been saved or not?"

"Well, I couldn't answer that. He is a lawyer, after all."

Sister Ora covered her mouth with hands folded in prayer and took a deep breath. "Say he is? Oh my. How awful. A lawyer. In that case, he probably isn't ready for his trial before the Great White Throne and probably won't ever be either, poor thing."

Dixie snickered. "What lawyer is ever ready for court, whether down here or up there? I've never known one to be. Especially that one lying there. He's never, ever been ready to try anything but somebody else's patience."

I started to say something, but I didn't. I wanted to hear what else Dixie might have to say about me, and I wanted to know more about this kidney cancer my visitor said I had.

Sister Ora continued. "Somebody, then, better help him understand we're all just one heartbeat away from eternity, you know. If they don't, he really is one doomed soul, him being a lawyer and all."

She tiptoed away from my bed and peeked around the curtain at my roommate. "That boy there on the other side of the curtain. . ."

"What about him?"

"I come by here this morning after the doctor got done with him. I hear tell he was in here for gunshot. Some woman shot him on the dance floor in a honky-tonk."

"Is that right?"

"Well, that may be why they brought him here, but that's not all there is to it. They're not telling the family everything. Not right yet, they're not."

"Really?"

"No, ma'am, they're not. Poor boy, he's got an old cannnn . . . cer. It's a cannnn . . . cer of the shoulder blade."

"What's that you say, lady?" my roommate cried out in a loud, anxious voice. "They say I've got me a cancer? Shoulder-blade cancer? Did somebody really say that?

How come ain't nobody told me? Are they gonna have to operate on me and they ain't told me nothing 'bout this? Did the bullet cause it? It have a cancer germ on it? What? Somebody tell me something. Oh, me. Oh, me. Please, somebody help me." Then he started bawling.

"I expect I better go get the nurse," Sister Ora said in a sweet, kind voice, but speaking faster. "Poor fella, he sounds a mite upset. Nice to meet you, honey. Tell your friend or whatever he is to you when he wakes up I'll be praying for him." She nodded toward the curtain. "Him there on the other side too. Bless his heart. Bless both their hearts. Nice meeting you."

And away she flew.

It took the nurses with the help of a doctor almost a half hour to calm my roommate down and convince him he didn't have shoulder-blade cancer or cancer of any kind. They also tried to assure him that bullets didn't carry cancer germs.

But how could they know that, I asked myself, *if they don't know what causes cancer anyway—well, what causes most cancers?*

When he dropped by later to see about me, Dr. Cohen laughed when I asked if there might be anything to what Sister Ora said about my condition. He told me not to worry, saying Sister Ora thought all patients had the disease. "But if it'll make you feel any better, Mr. Meek," he said with another laugh, "she boasts of a ninety-five percent cure rate by virtue of her visits and prayers."

His saying that made me feel worse, if anything. Assuming the accuracy of Sister Ora's figures—which Dr. Cohen did not gainsay, that meant five percent of the patients she visited and prayed for did in fact have cancer.

After Dixie left for the evening to go to her motel room, a nurse came in to prepare my roommate and me for the night. The whole time she worked on the two of us my roommate, notwithstanding what the nurses and doctor had told him, carried on again about maybe having cancer.

He kept on about it so I kinda wished he did have it and it'd be a really fast-acting one so I could get some peace and quiet.

I don't know what the nurse gave us because, thank the good Lord, my roommate shut up the moment she closed the door to our room. As for me, the next thing I remember was along about daylight I needed to use the urinal. I almost began the kidney stone retrieval process without the strainer; but I remembered to use it just before I got underway.

And it was good thing too. There in the middle of the strainer was a small, brownish little thing—something no bigger than a grain of sand. I had given birth to a kidney stone. I emptied it into my hand and held it between my fingers, marveling at it and wondering how something that small could cause so much pain and discomfort.

I decided to give my creation a name. The name I deemed the most fitting? I chose the name "Little Dixie."

CHAPTER ELEVEN

The doctor discharged me after taking one more X-ray and writing me a prescription for an antibiotic. We left for Abilene soon after I settled with the hospital and the urologist. It was a good thing I had brought traveler's checks along or I would've been required to hock my truck to pay each one—and I sure wouldn't have wanted to do that, not in a million years.

We arrived in Abilene around one o'clock and located the Star Lite Motel, a place someone in Weatherford had recommended to Dixie. It proved to be an attractive and relatively inexpensive motel with a nice swimming pool—which was of no use to me since I couldn't swim. After we registered for our rooms, the first thing I did when I got to mine was to check the telephone book to see if it carried a listing for a Roda Anne Harrison. It didn't—not even an R.A. Harrison. For some reason, nothing is ever easy for me.

Shortly afterward, Dixie and I rode over to the Conoco Truck Stop nearby for a quick bite at its restaurant. When we sat down at the table, she asked me whether I still felt any pain or discomfort.

"Feel fine," I told her.

"You sure?"

"I reckon I oughtta know how I feel. Why?"

"I mean, are you really sure?"

Something didn't seem right, her questioning me about my medical condition now that I no longer was under a doctor's care. "What is it you're just dying to tell me, Dixie? Come on out with it."

"Well," she said, raising and lowering her shoulders, "when I got to my room, you know what I did?"

"Let's see. You used the bathroom."

She gave me a disgusted look. "No, Mr. Smarty Pants. I mean after that."

"You got me."

"I looked in the phone book to see if it had a number and an address for the Harrison woman."

"How brilliant. I did that too."

She continued. "When I didn't see any, I called Billy Joe to see if Bible happened to be in. He was. In fact, he answered the phone. Said he'd taken my place. I told him that'd be the day."

Bible was the nickname of Billy Joe's investigator, James Mordecai Unthank. He'd retired from the Army where he'd served as a criminal investigator most of the time. He earned the nickname because he could recite Bible verses at the drop of a hat. Dixie and he were distant cousins.

"What'd you want him for?" I asked.

"I figured maybe he might have some ideas about how we could go about finding the Harrison woman. And he did. He suggested we get hold of some old phone books and city directories—to start there. He said we might find some at the local library, that sometimes they'd keep them on file. He said we also might check records that might list residents, like customer lists of public utilities—you know, a gas or electric company, propane dealers and the like. He said didn't everybody have a telephone. He said not to forget to check at the courthouse and the police agencies. He said, if we ever found a place where she once lived, we should remember *Matthew* 7:7."

"*Matthew* 7:7?" I said, not being familiar with the verse.

"I looked it up in the *Gideon Bible* there in the room after I hung up the phone. It said something to the effect that whenever we find whatever we're looking for, then we should knock—I guess on a door—and everything'll be made clear. Anyway, I was thinking after we get finished here, we might oughtta go find out where the library is."

"All right," I said. "That's what we'll do. We can start with the 1961 phone book. We know she was here in Abilene four years ago, judging from the postmark on that Christmas card—the one without a return address on it. Of course, she could've just mailed it from here. Could've just been passing through, doncha know."

Dixie took a sip of her tea, wiped her mouth, and shifted around in her chair. "Now, you're sure you feel okay?"

That was the second time she'd asked me about the state of my health. "Just come on out with it, Dixie."

"Okay, but I wanted to make sure you were all right before I tell you something—something you're not gonna like."

"Tell me what?"

"I also talked to Billy Joe. I'm afraid I've got bad news for you. The Phillipses, they've sued the colonel's estate. He wants you to call him tonight at home."

I tried not to show any reaction. I had expected them to bring suit eventually, but I had hoped they'd wait until I returned from Texas.

Dixie tilted forward and studied me for a moment. She leaned back and folded her arms. "You don't seem at all concerned."

"In fact, you're right. I'm not concerned about it at all. Not one little bit. I'm kinda glad they did it, actually. We'll find the person we're looking for, we'll return home, me and Billy Joe, we'll answer the complaint, we'll defend the case, try it in the probate court, and we'll get paid for doing it, whether we win it or not and whether we find Roda Anne or not. With them bringing suit—me myself—I've nothing to lose and lots to gain. Billy Joe, he does too."

Dixie grunted. "Lawyers."

"Yeah, 'lawyers.' Nobody likes them—not until they need one, doncha know."

"Don't kid yourself, Deloris. They don't even like them then," Dixie said, "especially if they happen to lose their case for them. Then it turns to hate."

* * * * *

We found the library on Cedar Street without any difficulty. While Dixie researched the telephone directories and the newspaper archives for a five-year period beginning in 1959 and ending in 1963, I concentrated on the city directories for that same period, starting with *Polk's Abilene (Taylor County, Texas) City Directory, 1961*. After neither of us had any luck in finding any mention of the Harrison woman during that time, Dixie suggested we go back a few more years. I agreed.

More time went by and right as I was about tell Dixie let's call it a day at the library and go examine the records at the courthouse and sheriff's office, Dixie said to me "Looka here what I've found in this 1958 phone book."

"What?" I said.

"Just for the heck of it, I decided to look to see if there was a listing for a Roda Anne Loomis—you know, see if she might've gone by the colonel's last name. And what do you know, there is. It's an address on Anson Avenue. Think we oughtta go out there and see if there's any connection to a Roda Anne Harrison?"

"Well, yeah, let's do it even if it doesn't pan out. What else have we got to show for our efforts today?"

We started gathering up the books and other things we'd borrowed. "After we get done here," I said, "let's go ask somebody at the desk if they have a city map they'll let us look at, and then we'll go."

The map the woman at the desk got for us indicated the street we wanted lay near Hardin-Simmons University. We left the library, made the block, drove up to North 3rd

Street, took a right, went down to and turned left on Pine Street, and followed it on out.

The Anson Avenue neighborhood appeared to be one populated by working-class people. It had no sidewalks. Power poles jumped from one side of the street to the other, but most stood on the southern side. Practically all of the houses were single-family dwellings of simple construction and design, many shaded by what I took to be Texas Oaks. Cyclone fences surrounded a few of the yards, and here and there we'd see an open field.

We came to the address listed in the phone book. The house sat on a treeless lot far back off the street. Painted a pale yellow and constructed of concrete blocks, the front of the dwelling had a small porch, a solid door shielded by a screen door, and two screened windows, both of which had been raised. A late model Dodge, its hood up and its right-rear tire flat, sat in the yard several feet from the front-door step. I pulled in next to the car, squeezing in between it and a discarded commode that sat upright in the yard.

I couldn't resist making a comment about the commode. "Look yonder, Dixie. Ain't that mighty nice of them? They must've known you were coming out this way and would be looking for a place to sit down, if you know what I mean."

Dixie didn't take the joke. "You know, Deloris, sometime I could just slap your jaws. I didn't make fun of you when you had that kidney stone. So, why are you making fun of me because of that bladder problem I had? And I might add, don't have now, but no thanks to you."

My face heated up. "Okay, you're right. I'm sorry." I turned off the ignition. "Tell you what, Dixie, I think you should be the one to go knock on the door."

"Me? Why me? You got two legs. You go."

I explained to her that a stranger with her good looks would be far more likely to obtain information from the occupant—man or woman—than a person who looked like me.

"You know," she responded, "for once in your life you've said something that makes a little sense. You'd probably scare the daylights out of them." And with that she opened the passenger-side door and dropped to the ground.

As she approached the door, a dog barked from deep inside the house. Dixie turned and cut her eyes at me while making a face.

I leaned out the window and motioned her forward. "Remember, Dixie, what Bible told you, *Knock on a door and all will be revealed*, or something like that."

She knocked. She waited. The dog barked again, but this time from closer range. Dixie whirled around and, her eyes wild-eyed, hurried down from the porch into the yard just as the main door opened.

An elderly, bearded man in a wine-colored housecoat and bedroom slippers stood on the other side of the screen door, an angry feist at his ankles, barking its little head off and baring its teeth. The man gave it a hard, swift kick, and the dog yelped and slinked off, its tail between its legs.

Dixie returned to the porch.

"Damn barkinest dog I ever did see," the man said in a loud voice. "One of these days I'm gonna shoot the damn thing. Damn sure am." He sized Dixie up with a leer and then stuck his head out from behind the door, glancing first one way and then the other. "If y'all here to try and collect some money I owe, ya'll're up the creek—way the hell up it."

"No, sir. We just wanna ask you something," Dixie said, using a reassuring tone as she returned to the porch.

The man closed the screen door but remained behind it. "Ask me something? Hell, I don't know nothing. Tell you something else too. I don't wanna learn nothing neither. Learning, it don't do nothing but mess your ass up. Whatcha don't know, it ain't gonna hurtcha. Another thing, you can't worry about whatcha don't know."

"Yes, sir."

"Well, what is it? I got cabbage cooking back yonder. Can't you smell it? Need to see after it directly, and that damn dog done crapped on the floor, and I gotta go clean it up too. Second time today he done it—the mean little bastard. Oughtta kill him, I tell you. I'm sure gonna do it, too, one of these days. Cephus Junior—that's my son—he don't believe me, but you just wait and see if I don't. Just let that dog do one more thing I don't like, and he's a gonner. Damn if he ain't."

I stepped out of the truck to go stand by Dixie. I smiled at the man as I approached. "How-de-do, sir, I'm Lawyer Deloris Meek, and we—"

Dixie interrupted. "We're looking for a lady by the name of Roda Anne Loomis or Harrison. We found out she might've lived here at one time. You wouldn't be related to her by any chance, would you, sir?"

"Naw, sure ain't. Name's Grubs. My wife, she was a Mitchell. Been dead going on sixteen years, my wife has. What I tell people is a bug done her in."

"A bug?" Dixie said. "The flu?"

"Oh naw. It happen when she was out riding on her Doodle Bug."

"Doodle Bug?" I said.

"You know, one of them little tiny scooters. She'd had it for three or four year. Rode it all the time, anywhere and everywhere. I told her she was gonna get herself killed one of these days, riding that thing. By crackie, if she didn't up and do it. Durn old pickup truck hit her. Slammed her up against a light pole, and one of its foot holds went slap, dab through her. Happened way, way before me and Cephus Junior moved here to Abilene. Driver, he didn't have no insurance or nothing. Never even said he was sorry. Blamed her, saying she run into him. She probably did.

"Funeral home what got her body, they wanted me to pay them nine hundred dollars before they'd bury her. You shoulda seen her. They had her body so made it, she look like a damn street-walker."

Grubs screwed up his face and shook his head. "Nine hundred dollars, my ass. I told them, *Well now, being she's deader'n a door nail, she don't belong to me no more. Mine and her contract, it's over and done with. Till death do you part—that sort of thing. Tell you what. Since y'all've got her now, she's all yours. Yessir, all yours. Like the fella told me one time, possession is nonsense of the law. So, y'all just go on ahead and do with her whatever y'all wanna do. I don't give a rat's ass whatcha do.* I turned myself around and walked on out, big as you please.

Finished, I thought, with his story, Grubs chest ballooned as he took a long, deep breath.

Dixie and I gave each other a look.

"Yes, sir," I said, "but what we—"

Grubs cut in, quashing my effort to put him back on track. "Later on, though, me and them at the funeral home, we worked out something other. What we done, see, was we torched her—you know, cremated her. Took some doing, but it got done. Didn't cost much neither. I mean, what's the price of a little propane or fuel oil or whatever the hell they use to do it with?"

"Yes, sir," Dixie said. "I'm sorry for your loss." She pointed at me. "We both are."

Grubs stroked his beard. "Well, it mightta been God's will. But then again, it mightta notta been."

"Yes, sir," Dixie said, smiling. "But getting back to Roda Anne Loomis or Roda Anne Harrison, would you happen to know either one of them by any chance, sir?"

"No, ma'am. Sure don't."

Dixie ran her fingers through her hair. "What about your son? Wonder if he might've heard of them?"

Grubs looked away for a moment and then back at us, wiping his mouth. "I dunno. But it wouldn't hurt none to ask him, I don't reckon."

He paused a moment, as if in thought.

"You know something? You mentioning my boy just now," Grubs continued, "that name Roda Anne, it does seem a mite familiar for some reason or other, come to think of it. It's kinda unusual—Roda Anne. Yeah, I remember now him saying something about a Roda Anne." Grubs chuckled. "Seems like when he said it I said something like, 'Roda Anne then what?' " He slapped his thigh and chuckled again. "Get it? Roda Anne then what? I tell you, now that's funny. I don't care what nobody says."

Dixie actually blushed.

If the old man noticed Dixie's reaction to his remark about our heiress' two given names, he sure didn't let on like it. Grubs repeated his little joke, turned, and put a hand to his mouth. "Cephus Junior. Oh, Cephus Junior," he called. "Come out here to the door a minute. Somebody wants to see you."

Grubs faced us again. "Cephus Junior, he's back yonder in his bedroom, watching the TV. He likes watching them kid shows." He squinted at me. "You really a lawyer?"

I swelled up. "Yes, sir. And a notary public," I said, emphasizing my answer with a nod.

"The hell you say?" He folded his arms and looked me over. "Your name's what now?"

"Deloris Meek."

Grubs' face broke into a wide grin, revealing open spaces that, up until then, his full lips and facial hair had concealed. "Why, my great grandma, her name, it was Delores too. She was an Elrod. Ain't that something else, now? Both y'all having the same name, and you being a fella too."

There was no sign of Cephus Junior, other than, perhaps, the faint sound of a television set coming from a room somewhere in the rear of the dwelling.

Grubs took a step back and turned to his left. "Cephus Junior. Cephus Junior," he called, louder than before. "Turn off that damn television and get your lazy ass out here. There's a lawyer needing some help, and he ain't just no regular lawyer neither. He's a noted republican too."

The sound of the television abruptly ceased. A few seconds later, a tall, slim man dragging his left foot came to the door and stood next to his father. He wore only a pair of boxer shorts and looked dreamy-eyed. "Whatsup?" he said, yawning and scratching his behind.

"They's asking about some woman named Roda Anne what might've lived here one time or another," the older man said. "You mentioned something about somebody by that name one time, but I can't recollect how it come up."

Cephus Junior blew his nose into his hand and wiped it off on the seat of his underpants. "I don't know if she lived here or not. I think she mightta've cause I found this box of love letters and other stuff one day right after we moved in when I was up in the attic, poking around. Some of them was addressed to a woman what went by that name—Roda Anne Sorrow."

My heart dropped. The last name was not the one I was looking for. It was not even close.

Cephus Junior continued. "They was in a shoe box what was all tied up with some red string. They was real sweet, them letters was, especially them what that Harrison boy wrote the Loomis girl. Why, I—"

I interrupted. "You say *Harrison*? And also *Loomis*, I take it?"

"Yes, sir. I used to shut the door to my room and read hisen over and over. Sometimes, I'd pretend I was one what wrote them to her."

His father pointed at his temple and twirled his index finger.

"So, I take it, Cephus Junior, that some of the letters are written to a woman named 'Sorrow' and some are written to one named 'Loomis.' Is that right?"

"And some to Roda Anne Harrison, too," Cephus Junior said.

My heart beat so hard against my chest I feared it my burst.

"How long have y'all lived here in this house?" Dixie asked.

Cephus Junior looked down at the floor a couple of seconds. "Not too long. What, two, three years, Daddy? Dunno exactly. I don't pay no attention to time no more."

"You still have the box, Cephus Junior?" she asked.

"The one what's got all them letters in it? Well, yessum. If y'all wait right here, I'll go fetch it for you. Won't take me but a second or two. Think I can recollect where I laid it at."

Cephus Junior limped away.

"Korea," his father said. "First Cavalry Division. He was an infantryman. Got hisself all shot up trying to help somebody. Now look at him. Damn government, it don't hardly do nothing to help me with him. He can't work or nothing. Bastards damn near blew his leg clean off. Can't tell you how long he was in the hospital and all. And if that wasn't bad enough, he come back here crazy as a june bug. Y'all seen that commode outside? He's the one tore it up. Now I ask you, how the hell do you tear up a damn commode? But he done it. Usually, though, he's pretty quiet. About all he does is watch the TV, sleep, and look after that little piss-ant dog of hisen."

"I'm sorry," Dixie said, dropping her head.

"Been better if he'd died. Ain't been worth a damn since he come back, but he can't help it none. I blame Harry Ass Truman. And that damn dog, it don't help none. Why, it's the barkinest, crappinest little bastard I ever heard tell of. Took up with Cephus Junior about three months ago. Ain't house broken or nothing. Every time I turn around good, it's done heisted its little leg and pissed all over on the floor or the furniture, one. I'm damn sick and tired of it.

"Cephus Junior, he gets a measly little old government check. Otherwise me and him'd done both starved our tails off, what with that and the little bit I get from the government—my social securitum. What he upped and started spending on food for that mangy dog, why, he could've bought us some nice steaks with ever now and then. Ain't been no steak in this house since it come crawling up here, whining and wanting something other to eat.

"Me? I got heart trouble, but don't nobody give a damn. Don't see me whining, though. Hell with everybody, I say—especially Harry Ass Truman, sending my boy over to some country ain't nobody never heard of before to get hisself all shot up. And he fired General MacArthur, too, the stupid bastard. Next to Robert E. Lee, the best damn general there ever was."

Grubs' rant ended when Cephus Junior returned with the box. He handed it to Dixie.

"Mind if I take this to the truck so me and Mr. Meek can sit and look through them, Cephus Junior? I promise we won't do anything to them, and we'll return them good as new before we leave."

"Yessum. That'll be all right. It don't matter none no ways. I don't pretend no more. Well, every now and then, I do. You know, when I get to feeling lonesome. But since I got my dog, it ain't often I feel that way. He's my best friend, my dog is."

He paused and smiled. "I call him Zoro. That's cause of them black spots around his eyes, they kinda make him look like he's got a mask on. Doncha think so?" He frowned and cut his eyes at his daddy. "If anything should happen to him, I think I'd go crazy. Ain't no telling what I'd do then."

Grubs harrumphed. "Go crazy?"

Dixie and I returned to the truck. "Damn," I said as I held the door open for her. "That old man can sure talk."

"He's not the only one," she responded.

I think she meant me.

Once inside, Dixie opened the box and passed me a stack of the letters, keeping the rest of the contents for her own review.

In addition to letters addressed to the Roda Anne, we found the box also contained what appeared to be some official papers or documents, news clippings, photographs, and the like.

I examined the topmost envelope and the letter inside. "Bingo, Dixie. Bingo."

Her eyes widened. "What?"

"This one here. The very first one. Look," I said, waving the letter, "It's from William Howard Taft Loomis. That's my man."

We further examined the box. I was determined to have everything in it of relevance or, at the very least, photocopies of those items.

While Dixie waited in the truck, I returned to Cephus Junior. I asked him what he'd take to allow me to copy what I wanted out of the box. Much to my surprise, he said he would sell me the box and all the stuff inside it for twenty dollars. I couldn't pay him fast enough. For a brief moment, I feared I may have seemed too eager.

After I handed him two ten-dollar bills, the old man said, "Well good. Maybe tonight we can eat better than that damn dog for a change. I sure would like to have me a nice

T-bone steak smothered in lots of onions and green peppers. And maybe some French-fries to go with it. Mmmmm-uh. Wouldn't you, Cephus Junior?"

"I don't know, Daddy," Cephus Junior replied, "I'm getting kinda low on dog chow."

I returned to the truck. As I backed out onto the street, a gunshot went off from inside the house. A sharp cry of a dog followed.

I thought, *Zoro*!

Dixie must've heard it, too, because she said, "Daddy'll be eating steak tonight. Whatcha wanna bet?"

Once I shifted into first gear, I pointed the truck in the direction of town. It gave a violent jerk when I pressed down hard—maybe a little too hard—on the accelerator. As I drove away, Dixie reached over and touched my right arm while looking out the passenger-side window back toward the Grubs' house. "Deloris, you hear that?"

"Hear what?"

"I dunno. Something. It was kinda a muffled sound. Another gunshot maybe?"

"I didn't hear anything. You probably heard something fall down in the back. Things are always slipping loose in there and winding up smack dab on the floor."

"Maybe so."

* * * * *

Dixie and I grabbed a couple of hamburgers for supper and retired to my room to examine the material in the box I bought from Cephus Junior. We separated the pictures, news clippings, letters, documents, and so forth from each other and then arranged them in an order of some sort. From there, we made a written outline, supplementing the information we gleaned from the box contents with things I already knew about the good colonel.

At one point, I handed Dixie a news clipping and its accompanying picture that announced Roda Anne Loomis' marriage to PFC Bobby Wayne Harrison. "Take a look at this. I know you never saw him in person, but I think Roda Anne kinda favors the colonel. We might could use this as evidence in the probate court."

Dixie withdrew from the shoe box an early photograph of the colonel taken when, judging from his uniform, he was in the Army Air Corps. She compared his image with that of his judicially declared daughter. "You asking my opinion?" she asked. "If so, I wouldn't use it if I were you. They don't look a thing alike. Not to me, they don't."

She tossed the clipping and photograph back into the shoebox. "Are we through for the night? I'm kinda tired."

"I guess. But there's one more thing I want you to do for me," I said.

"What?" She sounded irritated.

"Call Bible and ask him to use his Army connections to run down where we might find Bobby Wayne Harrison at. I wrote down his serial number on this piece of paper here." I handed her the paper. "I got it off a return address on an envelope he used to send his new mother-in-law a thank-you note for something she gave him."

"Wouldn't he be outta the Army by now?"

"Probably, but not discharged. I'm assuming he was inducted in either 1959 or early 1960 and did his two years as a draftee. He'd still owe the Army six more years, but he'd probably do his time in the Ready Reserves. On the other hand, he could've re-upped after his initial enlistment. Chances are, though, he didn't. Few do."

"How you know he was a draftee?"

"By his serial number. It uses the initials 'US.'"

Dixie yawned. "Okay. I'll let you know tomorrow morning what he says, assuming I can reach him. But one thing for sure, I'm not calling him tonight. I'm hitting the sack." She stood. "What time you wanna meet for breakfast?"

"Six o'clock?"

"No, eight."

I stared at her for a few seconds. "Why'd you ask me if you were dead set on meeting at eight?"

"Just wanted to know. Why?"

"Sometimes, Dixie, you don't make a damn bit of sense," I groused.

CHAPTER TWELVE

The very first thing I did the next morning was to hire a nice lady in the Star Lite's office to type up our handwritten outline. Dixie had gone over it with a fine-tooth comb and pronounced it "perfect, absolutely." With that out of the way, Dixie and I drove over to the Dixie Pig on Butternut Street where I pigged out on hash browns, biscuits and gravy, and eggs and sausage. Dixie made do with a cup of coffee and a piece of plain toast, saying she was watching her figure.

This prompted me to say, "You're not the only one watching it."

"Yeah," she said, "I know. And that's exactly why I'm doing it, smarty."

When we returned to the motel, I dropped by the office to check on the outline. The lady had finished with it, telling me she had found and corrected a few more errors. Dixie wasn't perfect after all, it seemed—certainly not absolutely perfect.

Here's how the outline read:

    1. Roda Anne Sorrow is born in Oklahoma in 1922, probably of Cherokee descent. Her mother, the former Roda Anne Waite, names the child after herself.

    2. Roda Anne Sorrow moves to Wichita Falls, Texas, before the start of World War II where she meets William Howard Taft Loomis, then a glider mechanic trainee at what is then called Sheppard Field.

    3. At age twenty, Sorrow marries Loomis on August 29, 1942,

just before the Army transfers Loomis on September 11, 1942, east to Laurinburg-Maxton Army Air Base in North Carolina. Sorrow remains in Wichita Falls where she works as a waitress at a local diner. Loomis mails the bulk of the correspondence he writes to Sorrow while stationed at either Sheppard or Laurinburg-Maxton.

4. Roda Anne Loomis, named after her mother and maternal grandmother, is born on June 17, 1943. Her mother claims the birth was overdue.

5. Loomis suffers a work-related accident in October 1943, in which he mangles two fingers on his left hand. The accident renders him incapable of performing work as a glider mechanic. The Army gives him a medical discharge, and Loomis returns to Texas. On the way back from North Carolina, however, he learns of an auctioneer's school in Indiana and enrolls in a three-week course in auctioneering. Among other things, he learns how to organize and manage an auctioneering business, how to chant and call for bids, and how to appraise both personal and real property.

6. He arrives home on Christmas Eve 1943 and within days rents a small office and sets up an auctioneer business. He begins to

refer to himself as "Colonel Loomis," in the tradition of auctioneers throughout the country.

7. Loomis files for a divorce several months after coming home, alleging adultery on the part of his wife with Clay Sedbury. In a decree dated January 12, 1944, which Loomis does not appeal, the judge holds Roda Anne Sorrow Loomis, the wife, guilty of adultery and holds Loomis is the father of the child Roda Anne Loomis notwithstanding his wife's adultery. The judge bases his opinion on the common-law presumption of legitimacy since the child was born during the marriage and Loomis had access to his wife during the gestation period. The judge also finds blood tests given the parties and the child do not exclude Loomis from being the child's father.

8. Following the divorce, Loomis relocates his business along the eastern seaboard; and in 1950, he marries Kathleen Robertson Hammonds, a wealthy widow whom he met six months earlier at a land auction and who owns a plantation named Grind Stone. Hammonds dies in 1962 and leaves her entire estate to the colonel.

9. In July 1960, Loomis' daughter Roda Anne Loomis marries U.S. Army Private First-Class Bobby Wayne Harrison, a native of Taylor

County, Texas. Abilene is the county seat of Taylor County. At the time, Harrison served as a musician with the 98th Army Band at Fort Rucker, Alabama. Roda Anne later joins him in Alabama.

10. Loomis dies in August 1965 and leaves his entire estate to his daughter, Roda Anne Loomis Harrison.

11. His ex-wife and daughter probably once lived at the Anson Avenue address in Abilene, maybe as late as 1960 and even as late as 1961.

The second I walked into my room I heard the phone ring. It was Bible. He called to tell me that a contact of his at the Department of the Army had found and given him an address and telephone number for Bobby Wayne Harrison. Although no longer in the Army, he remained in Alabama, residing in Ozark, a small town near Fort Rucker.

I had Dixie place a long-distance call to the number, figuring the person at the other end would deem me more credible if my "secretary" made the call for me. We got lucky. We caught Bobby Wayne at home before he left for work.

"Mr. Harrison," Dixie said after Harrison identified himself, "would you please hold for Attorney Deloris Meek?" There was a brief pause. "No," Dixie said with a slight laugh, "Attorney Meek is not a woman." There was another pause. "Yes, I know," she said, "but that's his name nevertheless. Here he is."

Dixie handed me the phone, rolling her eyes.

"Mr. Harrison, thank you for taking my call. But we're really looking for your wife, Roda Anne."

I learned from my conversation with Harrison that his wife worked as a bookkeeper at a local glass dealer. He, on the other hand, held a part-time job at a haberdashery and played piano for a gospel group who called themselves the "Center Cross Quartet." I made arrangements with him for me to telephone his wife that evening after work. He wanted to know why I needed to speak to her. All I would tell him was, "It's a legal matter."

Dixie and I checked out of the Star Lite, filled the gas tank up, and headed east within an hour of my conversation with Harrison. We drove for about six hours or so, stopping only for a quick bite to eat, some gasoline, and, of course, a rest stop or three until we reached Mineola, Texas, a small town on U.S. Highway 80 with an attractive main street.

We checked into a hotel; but before we looked for a place to eat supper, I had Dixie telephone the Harrisons from my room.

A woman answered the telephone. I spoke with her after Dixie confirmed her identity.

"Mrs. Harrison," I began, "as my secretary—"

"You wish," Dixie muttered.

"What's that?" Roda Anne said.

I made a face at Dixie. "Oh, nothing," I said, "as I was saying, as *my* secretary told you, I'm a lawyer. I represent the Estate of William Howard Taft Loomis."

"Loomis, you say?"

"Yes, Colonel Loomis. His estate."

"You said *Estate.*" She spoke in a guarded manner.

"Yes, ma'am. He passed recently—in August. To get right to the point of this call, his will named me the executor of his estate. I'm the estate's lawyer as well. I've been searching for you almost from the day he died. I believe, ma'am, you are his daughter. Am I right?"

A silence followed.

"Mrs. Harrison? You still there?"

"Sir, if you're calling, wanting money or something—"

"Oh, no. It's nothing like that," I hastened to say.

"Well, whatever it is you want, you should know I never saw or heard from him that I can remember. You say I'm his daughter. That's funny because he always denied being my daddy. In fact, he abandoned me as a baby and moved east to get away from me and my mama."

"Yes, ma'am. But didn't you try to contact him at one time?" I said, alluding to the Christmas card she had sent him in 1961.

She groaned. "It was more than once. I started trying to get up with him when I got older. That's the truth. When I found out where he was—Mama'd come across this listing of auctioneers—I'd send him Christmas cards, but I never heard anything back from him. Not a single time. Sent him a copy of my wedding announcement. Still didn't hear anything.

"I think the last card I sent to him was right before Mama died. I put a note in there telling him how sick she was. I'd come back home to help her. My husband, he couldn't get leave and come with me. He was still in the Army here in South Alabama—at Fort Rucker.

"Mama died on the second of January, 1962, not ever hearing from him or anything. I just didn't try to get in touch with him no more after that, it hurt me so."

"Let me ask you this," I said. "Did you leave a forwarding address at the Post Office when you returned to Alabama?"

"I don't think I did. It wasn't my permanent address. So, no, sir, I didn't. I doubt if it even crossed my mind to do it. I had so much to do right then. Making funeral arrangements, running down Mama's landlord, contacting this person and that, all sorts of things."

"I can well imagine," I said. I readily sympathized with the problems she faced at that time. Closing out a person's life is no easy task, especially a loved one.

I looked across the room at Dixie. She sat on the edge of my bed, staring at me with the words "I wanna know what she's telling you" etched all over her pretty face.

"You mentioned, Mrs. Harrison, that you sent him a Christmas card shortly before your mother died. That'd be the one you sent him in 1961. Well, I found it."

"You did?" she said.

"Let me ask you this. Why didn't you put a return address on it?"

"You mean I didn't?"

"No, ma'am. Maybe that's why you didn't hear back from him."

Her end of the telephone went silent. I thought for a moment we'd been disconnected.

"Mrs. Harrison?" I said.

"Oh, I'm sorry, Mr. Meek. I can't think of any reason why I didn't put one on it. I guess I must've forgot. How stupid of me. But I'm sure I put one on other things I'd sent him, either Mama's Texas address or my Alabama one. I'm pretty sure I did, but maybe I didn't. I just don't know."

"Well, who knows what he did with them. I just know I searched for your address among his private effects, and all I came up with was the 1961 Christmas card. I was lucky even to find that."

"He probably threw my letters away the moment he got them," she said. Her voice seemed to choke. "Excuse me a second, Mr. Meek."

I covered up the mouthpiece and whispered to Dixie, "She's crying or starting to."

A moment or so later she continued our conversation.

"I think it took Mama's death to make me realize what was obvious to her and everybody else—you know, that he didn't want anything at all to do with me. I didn't try and send him anything else after that.

"Why should I? He didn't think I was his young'un, though Mama swore to me on the Bible he was, and that was good enough for me. Mama was a Christian, and she wouldn't swear to no lie, not on the Bible, she wouldn't. Yes, she made a mistake, but that other man wasn't my daddy. And God forgave her for that, and if God forgave her, my daddy, he should have too, but he didn't.

"So, I don't guess it mattered that he never saw fit to write me back or thank me or nothing for my cards and letters. He wasn't a father to me anyway. I hate talking bad about the dead, but that's how it was, Mr. Meek. And if he's burning in Hell right now on account of how he treated me and Mama, I don't really care. I sure don't."

I thought it time to get to the point. She no longer seemed to be crying.

"Mrs. Harrison, ma'am, like I told you, I'm not calling to ask you for money. Just the opposite. This may come as a big surprise to you—I'm calling to tell you that you have come into a sizeable inheritance. You are now the owner of Grind Stone Plantation and a whole lot more."

When I got no response of any kind, I repeated what I'd told her and added, "Mrs. Harrison, he must've cared for you somewhat, don't you think? To leave you all that."

An unmistakable sound of crying now came over the line. I held the phone to my ear for I don't know how long.

Finally, the crying stopped. "Mr. Meek, I'm sorry. I don't know what to say. I'm overcome, frankly speaking," Roda Anne said with a weak voice broken with sniffs. "I just can't believe what's happened. I just can't. I hope this is not some kind of joke, because if it is . . ."

I told her I fully understood her feelings and doubts right then. I went on to relate how I had met the colonel, drafted his will, and attended to his funeral arrangements. I also told her of my efforts to locate her. I saved the worst part—the lawsuit business—for last.

She offered to cooperate in every way, and I promised to keep her fully informed. When I told her I had to hang up, she began crying again, almost to the point she could barely tell me goodbye.

For once in my career as a lawyer, I felt really, really good about performing a legal service.

"So why the big grin?" Dixie asked after I returned the telephone to its cradle.

I told her pretty much all Roda Anne had said and described how excited she had become at the news of her good fortune.

"Wait till she gets your bill. She won't be so happy then, I bet."

* * * * *

We found a nice, quiet restaurant downtown just a few doors up from our hotel. I figured it'd be an all-right place to eat at since it had white tablecloths. I ordered a T-bone steak while Dixie asked for "the catch of the day." That turned out to be frozen flounder. When she complained to me about how she'd been misled, I asked her how they could have possibly done that. I pointed out to her that they hadn't said anything about who'd caught it, where it was caught, and what'd happened to it after it was caught.

She was not pleased that I seemed to defend the restaurant, but I was only trying to get her to liven up.

My steak wasn't anything to write home about either. I learned that night I shouldn't allow the presence of white tablecloths and cloth napkins to influence my decision regarding where I should dine. The fact that we were the only customers at seven o'clock in the evening should've been a clue that something wasn't exactly right.

Each of us tried our very best to make the most of the situation, however—although my jaw hurt all night long from the effort I made to grind the meat between my molars sufficiently enough for me to swallow it without choking to death. I also took the opportunity to ask Dixie something I'd wanted to know ever since we had left Baggett, back in our home state.

I took a sip of my ice tea, wiped my mouth, and cleared my throat. "Dixie," I said, "I got a question for you."

She picked at her fried flounder, ignoring the baked potato that came with it. "What?" she said, without looking at me.

"Now, I know it's none of my business—"

"Then don't ask me," she said glumly.

"How come you didn't lemme drop you off in Baggett?"

She continued to poke at her fish, moving it around on her plate.

"I'd offer you some of my steak, Dixie, but it might break that pretty jaw of yours if you tried to eat it."

She raised her head, looked me in the eyes, and smiled. "All right. I'll tell you. But don't you say a word to Billy Joe about it, you hear me? I know how y'all talk about me."

"We don't do no such a thing, Dixie," I said, somewhat offended, although she told the truth.

"Uh-huh. Right." She set her fork to the side. "The reason I wanted to go to Baggett was I'd gotten a letter that my high school graduating class was having its fifth-year class reunion. Also, it'd give me a chance to do something I probably should've done years ago, and that was to try and make up to my father."

"Your dad lives in Baggett?"

She bit her lips and clasped her hands together as she laid them on the table. "I ran into somebody recently, and they told me he was in a bad way. That kinda put me on a guilt trip.

"Then that letter came about the reunion. I sent them the money and told them I'd be there. I believed then it was the right thing to do to try and see him, especially after I learned you'd be going through there on your way to Texas. I planned on staying with him, if he'd permit it.

"But the closer we got to Baggett, the more I began to have second thoughts. Plus, I was sick with a bladder problem, but didn't really realize it. I was feeling bad, really bad."

Dixie had now succeeded in putting me on a guilt trip.

She continued with her story. "So, I started to rethink about what I was up to. I mean, there were Mama's feelings I had to consider too, wondering how she'd take my going to see him—you know she lives with me. Daddy used to beat her just about every time he got drunk, which was pretty often. He couldn't hold a job because of his drinking, his alcoholism. Mama's the one who kept a roof over our heads, working there at Baggett Mill—the poor thing. Sometimes two shifts. I think what kept her going was she's one of those kinds of people that worries about any and everything. I mean, when anybody called the house—and I don't care who it was—as soon as Mama said hello and the caller spoke Mama would say, *What's wrong?*

"But getting back to Daddy, everybody knew about how sorry he was. I can't tell you how embarrassing, how humiliating it was to have a daddy like that. A truly awful man. There are worse things than not having a daddy, and one of them is having a daddy like I had."

"I'm sorry, Dixie. I didn't realize—"

She leaned back in her chair and dropped her head. "Oh, that's all right, Deloris. I feel like talking about it now. Anyway, like I was saying, I was wondering if I was doing the right thing in going back there. My high school years were the most miserable time of my life, to be honest. None of the decent boys ever once asked me for a date. I never went to a high school prom or anything like that—hayrides, football games, dances. I'd just sit home, watching TV or reading my magazines and books, dreaming about romance—that sort of thing. I think that's why I'm a sucker for love stories even today. Anyway, if I wasn't doing that, I'd be at some church function—like a prayer meeting or at choir practice, those kinda things."

"As pretty as you are and none of the boys wanted to date you, Dixie? I kinda find that hard to believe," I said.

"I said none of the decent ones wanted to. I wasn't about to go out with any of those lint-heads or clodhoppers. I didn't wanna wind up like Mama. And besides, I wasn't all that pretty. I didn't know how to fix my hair or my face or pick out clothes for myself. Then too, we were holiness, and we weren't supposed to use make up and stuff. We certainly weren't supposed to go to dances.

"Anyway, after I graduated, I left Baggett and enrolled in a business college where I learned shorthand, typing, and a little bookkeeping. I landed jobs here and there and got Mama away from Baggett soon as I was able. I wound up working for Dr. Lowe. Worked there until he got murdered. Then Billy Joe hired me."

To hear Billy Joe tell it, she hired herself.

"So that's my life in a nutshell. Not much there, and that's why I changed my mind about attending the reunion. There was nothing there for me except bad memories. Maybe if I had made something of myself I might've felt differently. You know what I'm saying? I mean, I knew there'd be some there that'd done something with their lives, gone to college or studying to be a preacher or had married well and become parents, had happy marriages—if there is such a thing. You know, stuff like that."

Dixie sat for a moment with a faraway look in her eyes. She caught herself and smiled at me. "You ever been to a class reunion, Deloris?"

"I went to high school one not long ago. That was something else, I'm here to tell you. One thing I remember happened, if you wanna hear about it."

"I do."

I looked around, leaned toward Dixie, and lowered my voice. "Well, there was this old boy who was the fullback on the football team. Boy, he was a good-looking fella. All muscle, not an ounce of fat on him any place. All the girls, they'd have fainting spells whenever he'd come walking by. He could've been a movie star, he was so handsome.

"Anyhow, I was standing there at the reunion, and all of a sudden the room kinda shook. I looked up, and here comes these two really big people tramping into the room. I mean they were huge, really huge. When he got closer, I got a good look. His face seemed familiar, and then it dawned on me who it was. It was Charles Foster Cleaver—we called him 'Meat'—you know, not because he was fat or nothing, it was on account—"

"It goes with Cleaver," Dixie said, finishing the sentence for me. "I get it."

"But now, he must've weighed three hundred pounds or more. His wife more than that, if you can believe it. So, I said to him after some small talk, *Meat, where y'all living at now?* He told me they lived some place in Northwest Florida."

"I asked him what he did for a living. Know what he said?"

Dixie shook her head.

"He said him and his wife, they ran a donut shop."

She laughed. "I guess that explains it." She pushed her chair back from the table and crossed her legs. "Where'd you go to high school?"

"Went to a country high school. You probably never heard of it. It was so country that we didn't catch the school bus. Naw, we caught the school mule."

Dixie laughed again, this time so hard the cashier frowned at us. I don't know why he did that because Dixie and I were the only customers in the place.

"I wanna ask you something really personal, since you asked me something like that," Dixie said, her eyes twinkling and an open lip smile on her face.

I told her to go ahead and ask it.

"Don't you have a middle name you could've used instead of 'Deloris'? People are always thinking you have a girl name. I know you get tired of having to explain it."

I managed a weak laugh. "Yeah, but it's just as bad."

I remembered the conversation I had had about my middle name in Shreveport and how a little bit afterward I got my tail whipped but good.

"Really? What is it?" Dixie said. "I don't think I ever heard you or anyone else say."

"My other given name?" I paused and gritted my teeth. "It's 'Ursel.' It's a name I think means 'bear.' "

A quiet followed as we sat, our eyes fixed on one another.

Then Dixie did something unexpected. She smiled, bent forward, reached across the table, and patted the top of my hand. "Thank you," she said, speaking softly.

"For what?" I said, somewhat taken aback by her action.

"For such a wonderful evening." She withdrew her hand. "And one other thing before we go. I like your name. There's a certain sweetness to it."

Dixie laid her napkin onto the table and scooted back in her chair, prompting me to get up and rush around to the other side of the table to help with her chair. Before I could step to the side, Dixie turned and kissed me on the cheek—a kiss that left me disoriented, if not completely undone.

* * * * *

I called Billy Joe when I got back to my room to let him know where we were and to find out a little bit more about the law suit. I told him of my conversation with the Harrison woman. All he wanted to know about, though, was Dixie. He sounded rather anxious and even a little jealous that I'd spent all this time with her. Of course, I didn't breathe a word about what Dixie had disclosed to me at dinner about herself.

I did manage, however, to learn the principal basis of the Phillipses' claim against the colonel's estate. They alleged I had used undue influence on the colonel and, because of that, he'd disinherited them and named Roda Anne Harrison his sole heir instead. My first reaction to what Billy Joe told me was to wonder how in the world they could ever prove such a thing.

Then he told me the Phillipses had decided not to use Meriwether Suffridge, IV after all, either that or Suffridge had refused to handle their case once he'd investigated it. The lawyer who served the complaint for the Phillipses? Oleander "Smudge" Chiselbrook, so low down he needed to look up to see the belly of a snake. He was one lawyer that'd do anything—and I mean anything—to win a case. At least that was his reputation. Why he had not been disbarred remained one of life's greatest unsolved mysteries. It seemed like every time the grievance committee had the goods on him, something would happen, and he'd get off—witnesses would die, disappear, or be unable to remember things or documents would get lost or be corrupted somehow. Some people can get away with damn near anything—no matter what, and Smudge Chiselbrook was one of them.

"Smudge served you with the suit papers, Billy Joe?" I asked.

"Yeah, he did. I guess Meriwether must've said something to Smudge after the Phillipses decided not to use him. I had told Meriwether I'd accept service of the summons and complaint when we were thinking they'd employ him to bring suit. You know, as a courtesy." There followed a pause. "You're not upset I did that, are you?"

"Oh, no, no. You did the right thing. The quicker we get this thing underway, the quicker we'll get it resolved. And another thing. I much rather we go up against Smudge Chiselbrook that Meriwether Suffridge any day."

"Well, let's don't get over confident," Billy Joe said. "You know how lucky Smudge can get sometimes."

CHAPTER THIRTEEN

The morning after Dixie and I returned from Texas, I pulled into one of my three parking spaces next to Kingry Insurance. I sat for a moment, sipping my fourth cup of coffee and experiencing a mix of emotions. While happy to be home again, I treasured the time Dixie and I had spent together, investigating the whereabouts of Roda Anne Harrison and, having found her, then driving back home.

Upon reaching Dixie's apartment the night before, we had sat in my truck for a moment, each one of us making apologies for our selfish behavior during our trip west, particularly the first part of it. I had carried her luggage to the door and set it down when Dixie pecked me on the cheek. All the way to my place, I had fought to retain the feel of that small kiss for as long as I could. Although it had faded away in due course, the memory of it remained with me for ages.

Once I finished my morning coffee and returned to reality, I sauntered into Kingry Insurance to inquire of Mr. Kingry's secretary about any telephone calls that might've been made to me during my absence. Although I'd received several, only one really interested me—that from Smudge Chiselbrook.

I decided not to telephone Smudge right then. I called Billy Joe Pratt instead. I caught him with Dixie. He said she was filling him in on all that had happened, including things I hadn't mentioned when I had spoken with him while en route to Texas and once I got there.

"You've had quite an adventure, haven't you, old sport? You reckon that old coot really shot his son's dog? You know, the one there in Abilene?"

"Sounded to me like he did," I said. "I didn't bother to check. He might've gotten shot his own self, if what

Dixie heard when we left from there was another gun going off."

I agreed with Billy Joe that I'd had an interesting journey, particularly the evening I spent with Dixie in Mineola, Texas, something I didn't tell him about. I still hadn't gotten over how Dixie had acted toward me then and afterward, for that matter.

Once I ended my telephone conversation with Billy Joe, I decided to pay Smudge a personal visit at his office rather than telephone him. Billy Joe and I both agreed I should try to set up a conference in Billy Joe's office that afternoon aimed at negotiating a settlement of the action the Phillipses had brought against the Loomis' Estate and me. One thing all members of the local Bar knew about old Smudge, he'd settle anything for anything. All that was required was to dangle an offer in front of him, and he'd grab hold of it like a drowning sailor reaching for a life preserver.

I walked into his office, a one-floor, two-room building wedged between two high-rises. The building had once belonged to a watch repairman, but somehow Smudge had beat him out of it and acquired title to the property, much to the chagrin of the owners of his towering neighbors.

Smudge's secretary sat just inside the door behind what had once been a jewelry showcase, but now displayed only dust, some dead flies, a spider web or two, and an out-of-date J. C. Penney catalogue. Rock music played on a small radio as she, smacking gum, flipped through the pages of a *Life Magazine* with one hand while the other held a lighted king-size cigarette. A cup of steaming coffee rested on a metal table next to a manual typewriter, a beat-up Underwood.

She waited a moment before she acknowledged me by looking up and running her tongue over her full, pouting lips as my eyes got their fill. Rather than greet me with any words of salutation, she continued her performance, sucking in air that seemed to pump up her soft-ball size breasts like a couple of balloons and float them to new heights. Then, she smiled and sat gazing at me as if to say, "You want me, don't you?"

I know I blushed, but I had only reacted at the display of her cargo like any normal man my age would have done. There are some things a man just cannot help doing and staring at a beautiful woman is one of them, especially if she appears to be showing off.

To describe the young woman as a hot number would be an understatement. I could feel the heat from her body ten feet away. I am sure Smudge hired her for reasons other than her secretarial abilities. From what I had seen of her work, she possessed the typing skills of a blind, one-fingered orangutan fresh out of the jungle. As I indicated, she wasn't exactly friendly to walk-ins. But that probably didn't matter because her comeliness made up for her frosty behavior. Yet as good-looking as she was, she couldn't hold a candle to Dixie St. John.

"Morning, Mavis," I said, "Smudge in?"

She ran her tongue over her lips again and took a draw of her cigarette. "No . . . he's . . . not," she whispered breathlessly through puffs of smoke from her Pall Mall.

I asked when she expected him.

She raised her shoulders and tilted her head to the left and reached for her coffee. She gazed at me through dreamy eyes and took a slow sip. I took that as a sign she hadn't a clue about where he was or when he'd be in—and, if the truth be known, could care less.

I figured the only logical place I might catch him would be at the city court where I could expect to find him shaking down loiterers, drunks, and the like, offering to represent them for whatever cash money they might happen to have in their pockets right then.

Sure enough, that's where I found him. I took a seat out in the audience to watch the proceedings. For the most part, they repeated themselves day after day involving, as they did, the same judges, the same lawyers, the same policemen, and, more often than not, the same defendants facing the same charges. Some lawyers referred to the court as the "Carousel."

Smudge stood in front of the bench with the city judge staring down at him with glassy eyes and listening to the same spiel Smudge had repeated over and over again almost every morning in city court, no matter the judge, no matter the client, and no matter what the client did or didn't do. A hand braced the judge's chin as Smudge droned on about what a fine Christian, God-fearing, church-going man his client was. Smudge had probably just met him five minutes before. Probably also, the man had been arrested for the umpteenth time for public drunkenness and the last time he had ever darkened the door of a church was to get warm, to get out of the rain, or get a free meal.

Just when it appeared that Smudge had concluded his remarks, the judge dropped his hand, sat up straight, and opened his mouth to say something. Before he could do so, however, Smudge got to the next verse, so to speak, as his client stood trembling next to him with his head held low. I suspected the trembling resulted more from the effects of alcohol than from any fright the poor devil might have had, Carousel veteran that I imagined he was.

"Your Honor," Smudge said, as he launched into the poor devil's allegedly hard upbringing, "my client here. Excuse me a second, Your Honor." Smudge leaned toward the man. "What's your name again?" he said in a whisper loud enough to be heard throughout most of the courtroom.

The defendant whispered something back to him, causing Smudge to wave a hand in front of his face.

"Oh, right," Smudge muttered.

Smudge pulled at his tie and continued. "My client, Henry Green, I mean, Brown—got my colors mixed up there, Judge—Henry Brown," he said with a laugh. "Yeah, Henry Brown, he's a fine man, Your Honor, when he ain't drinking. He grew up hard, he tells me. Says both of his parents, they were drunks and no count. He just learned from them. Sure did. Started drinking when he was knee-high to a grasshopper. What he said. We can't blame him for his drinking, no we can't. There but for the grace of God. He didn't have the upbringing me and you had, Your Honor. He quit school when he was nine and went to work in the cotton fields. One time he was out there picking cotton and a snake bit him, and he ain't been right since then, he tells me. Has to drink to relieve the pain. Doctors, they can't do nothing for him. He—"

The judge interrupted. "Just a minute. What kinda snake was it, Mr. Chiselbrook?"

"What kinda snake? A cottonmouth, Your Honor."

"A cottonmouth, you say? Out in a cotton field, Mr. Chiselbrook? That's one lost snake."

The audience laughed.

Smudge enjoyed playing the role of court fool. All the city judges allowed him to get by with it. I even heard a judge comment one time that Smudge made an otherwise dreary court assignment something to look forward to. The downside for Smudge, though, was that his being permitted to clown around meant none of the judges ever took him serious about anything.

The judge let the laughter run its course, which it did in short order. He smiled and rolled his eyes. "Last fella you had up here, Mr. Chiselbrook, I believe you said a coach whip chased him down, got ahold of him, and almost whipped him to death."

The audience laughed again, as did the judge—probably because he provoked it.

"Yes, sir," Smudge said, "I did say that, Your Honor. I sure enough did. Awful thing, that was too. Sure gotta watch out for snakes these days. We're disturbing their habitats, they tell me."

The judge pushed back from his desk. "How about wrapping it up, Mr. Chiselbrook. I'm ready to sentence him. I have a bunch more cases to get to."

"Like I was saying, this copperhead, it come up and bit him out there when he was helping them harvest peanuts."

"What's that? I believe you said a moment ago he was out in a cotton field and it was a cottonmouth that bit him."

"I'm sorry, Your Honor. I got him mixed up with another client. Some of these cases, they kinda run together on me. Like I was about to say—"

The judge held up his hand. "I'm ready to sentence him now, Mr. Chiselbrook. So, just stand aside a moment. Let me ask your client a couple of things."

"Mr. Brown," the judge said, "when was the last time you were in my court? You remember?"

"Been quite some time, I'm thinking, sir."

"You've got a drinking problem. You know that, don't you?"

"Yes, sir. But it ain't as bad as it was."

"Remember what I gave you last time you were here?"

"Not exactly."

"Well, I'm sentencing you to the same thing today. Thirty days. Next case."

Smudge grinned. "Thank you, Your Honor. Appreciate it."

Smudge jumped to one side to allow another defendant and his lawyer to approach the bench. When Smudge turned around, I motioned to him. He smiled, hustled up the aisle, and plopped down next to me.

"Hey, Deloris," he said in a hushed voice, "heard you been all the way out to Texas."

"Yeah? Who told you that?" I whispered back.

"That's confidential information."

"The Phillipses told you, didn't they?"

"Damn! How'd you know that? Ain't nothing secret around here no more."

I shook my head. "Smudge, you sued my client—the Loomis' Estate. Don't you remember? It's only been a few days."

"Oh, that's right. Sure did."

I shook my head backward. "Can we step outside a second? I need to ask you something."

Smudge followed me out into the hallway, an area filled with people going and coming or simply hanging out.

"Hurry up, Deloris," Smudge said, taking a peek inside the courtroom through the small window of the hallway door. "I've got one more case."

Since he brought it up, I became curious. "How much did that last fella pay you, Smudge?"

He chuckled and scratched his cheek. "Him? Five dollars, I believe. Yeah. Five dollars."

"Is that all?"

"Well, yeah. Another one paid me seven, plus I got money coming from the next one. How much you made this morning?"

"I haven't made anything."

"All right. Well, I have. So there." He hiked his breeches. "Now whatcha want? I gotta get back on inside. Like I say, I still got one more left—and he ain't paid me yet. Not one dime. Wouldn't want the court to handle it without me being there. I'd never get my money if that happened."

I could've cared less even if what he said carried any truth to it whatsoever. "Smudge," I said, "it won't make a durn bit of difference whether you stand up there for him or not, and you know that as well as I do. He'll get the same exact sentence—thirty days."

Smudge looked at me in disbelief. "I ain't worried about no sentence. The time he gets, that's all his." Smudge slapped his wallet. "His money, whatever he's got, that's mine. Come on now, how about making it quick. Tell me whatcha want."

"I want you to do something. I want you to get hold of Bessie Phillips and her brothers and I want all y'all to meet me at Billy Joe's office this afternoon around four-thirty. Reckon you could do that?"

"For what?" He opened the door to the courtroom.

"To talk settlement."

He closed the door. "Settlement? You say settlement?"

"Settlement," I replied.

He grinned and rubbed his hands. "Allllll right. We'll be there with bells on—whistles too." He reopened the door. "Be there at four-thirty on the dot."

He hurried away, yelling out as he ran down the aisle, "Here I am, Judge. Here I am. Wait! Wait! Don't sentence him right yet. He ain't paid me yet."

* * * * *

Just as he promised, Smudge Chiselbrook and his clients—the Phillipses—arrived at Billy Joe Pratt's office at four-thirty. I'd beat them there by only a couple of minutes. When I walked in, Dixie hugged me—right in front of Billy Joe. He glowered at me but didn't say anything. He then motioned for me to follow him into his private office.

Before either of us could sit down, Smudge greeted Dixie in the outer office and, in a loud voice, introduced her to his clients. Dixie wasted no time in herding the four of them into Billy Joe's office toward the two of us.

Bessie Phillips ignored Billy Joe's outstretched hand, but each of her brothers shook it. I made no effort to shake any of their hands, including Smudge's. Dixie offered to get a soft drink or coffee for anyone. Only Smudge, as might be expected, took her up on the offer. While she went to get it, everyone found a seat in one of the several chairs Billy Joe had arranged in a circle.

Dixie returned with a twelve-ounce cola, apparently aware that Smudge would much prefer it to a smaller, six-ounce one—not because of its taste, but only because the larger contained more of the stuff. Smudge rejoiced in anything being given him without his having to earn it; and the more of it he got, the better. After serving Smudge and with everyone but Bessie watching her every move, Dixie drew up a chair, flipped open her dictation pad, and sat down.

Bessie spoke first. "Where's the so-called heir apparent? You'd think she'd be here."

Billy Joe answered for our side. "Mrs. Harrison? She's not coming. She couldn't get off from work, neither she nor her husband. And they live a good ways off. But don't worry. She and Mr. Meek have given me full authority to conduct these negotiations."

"Oh, I'm so disappointed," Bessie replied with a frown, "my brothers and I so much looked forward to meeting her—the little Jacoba."

The two brothers bobbed their heads in approval.

Billy Joe kinda laughed but turned business-like very quickly. "Smudge—Mr. Chiselbrook, to get right to the point, this is what we propose. We offer you the colonel's automobile, a late model Chrysler with only twelve thousand, eight hundred miles or so on it. It's clean as a whistle, got pretty good tires. Been serviced frequently, judging from the papers in the glove box."

Before Smudge could respond, Bessie blurted out, "Unacceptable. Unacceptable. We are here for one purpose only—"

Smudge interrupted. "What Miss Phillips is trying to say—"

"You, Sir, you shut up," Bessie said. "I will do the talking here. Understand me?"

Smudge shut up. I gathered he understood.

A quiet ensued and hovered about the room. It reminded me of the silence that met me when I visited the funeral parlor to check on Colonel Loomis' body and it was just the two of us in the viewing room. It wasn't so much a gloomy silence as it was an empty one.

"All right. You don't want the car, I take it," Billy Joe said after the silence had become almost unbearable.

"Bull's eye," Bessie said. "We want it all, and we intend to get it all, including the Chrysler. How's that grab you?"

"Yeah, that's right," Smudge added. "We've got us a surprise witness that'll help us get it, too." Smudge shifted around in his chair and flashed his big front teeth so that he reminded me of a smiling beaver.

Bessie made a face at Smudge and shook her head. She had just found out what every lawyer in town knew about Smudge. He was one of those lawyers who told everything he knew, including any confidential information disclosed to him by a client, no matter what it was.

Undeterred by Bessie's attempt to cut him off, Smudge kept on disclosing. "He saw whatcha did, Deloris—how you put all kinda pressure on the colonel and forced him to sign that stupid will of his." Smudge pumped the air with his raised fist and gritted his teeth. "He's our ace in the hole. Y'all ain't gotta chance of winning this case, not with him as our witness, and you know you don't."

I started to say something, but Billy Joe spoke before I could get it out. "Oh, really? And just who might that witness be, Smudge. Anybody we know?"

"That, sir, is none of your—" Bessie responded in a haughty voice.

Smudge, interrupting her, spilled the beans. "You'll find out anyway. It's Jerome Turbyfill, that's who. He witnessed the will, along with Jay Wyndam and some guy named 'Carl Trammel.' "

I remembered Turbyfill, a middle-aged man who, from the looks of him, lacked much in the way of smarts. As I recalled, he could barely sign his name when I pointed out to him where to sign on the colonel's will. I also remembered what Colonel Loomis had told me about Turbyfill's having been in trouble with the law and my being a little concerned about that at the time, but not enough to try to get someone else to be a witness.

Smudge continued to run his mouth. "Old Wyndam, he probably coulda help us too, but he up and got himself killed while Deloris was out there in Texas, playing cowboy. Man knifed him for fooling around with his wife. Killed him right outside the American Legion Hut. Stabbed him twenty-seven times." Smudge laughed. "Man told the police he kept stabbing him till he 'give out.' Sure did. What he said."

"Yeah," Billy Joe said, "I read about that."

"Can't find Trammel," Smudge said with a sigh. "Somebody told me they thought he wasn't from around here but was just somebody who come passing through, even though he put down on the will he was from around here. But I ain't given up on finding him—not by no long shot."

So, I now concluded, the case in all likelihood, would pretty much boil down to my word against Turbyfill's, a dumb ass with a minor criminal record. My confidence rose.

Smudge looked at Bessie and rubbed his hands. "I think we got us a strong case, especially when you consider ain't nobody never heard of this Harrison woman before now."

Billy Joe stood and stared a moment at Bessie Phillips who glared back at him, her mouth closed tight as a drumhead. "Okay then," he said, eyebrows raised. "I don't see where we're getting anywhere. I guess we'll see y'all in court. Thank you for coming."

Bessie motioned to her brothers. "Let's go. Didn't I tell you this would be a complete waste of time? You can't negotiate with thieves and co-conspirators."

The three hit the door, hurrying away in single file. Smudge stood to follow them and threw up his hands. "Sorry, Billy Joe. Done all I could."

Billy Joe stayed seated. "Well, if you say so."

Smudge held up the unfinished bottle of cola. "Mind if I keep this?"

Billy Joe waved him away.

"Before I leave y'all, could I say one more thing? Something that's been bothering me ever since I heard about it."

"Sure," Billy Joe replied.

Smudge nodded toward me. "Next time you're in my office, Deloris, I'd appreciate it if you wouldn't come on to my secretary like you done this morning when you dropped by there. Okay?"

"Say what, now?" I said, stunned at what he said. I didn't need to look at Dixie to gauge her reaction to Smudge's comment. I could sense it.

"Mavis said the second you walked in you started undressing her with your eyes. Said it embarrassed her near about to death."

I know my face shown crimson. I could feel it. "I did no such thing, Smudge."

Of course, I knew I was lying to some extent. I suspect both Smudge and Billy Joe knew that too. That's because there never lived a heterosexual male over the age of sixteen years who could simply *look* at Mavis and that'd be it. No, she required a stare at the very minimum.

I finally summoned the courage to glance over at Dixie. She stood, glaring at me with her arms folded and her foot tapping away as she's wont to do when agitated or irritated. I shook my head no, but it had no effect on her. She, too, knew better.

Smudge went right on with his allegation but in an understanding and nice tone of voice. "Course, I don't know, Deloris, if you done it or not. I wasn't there. But please don't do it no more if you did do it. I don't do it when I come to your office, you know."

"I reckon you don't," I said, feeling very much aggravated. "I don't even have a secretary."

"That's all I got to say. Just please leave her be next time. I know you will. She's kinda touchy about things like that—you know, sensitive."

He turned to leave. "Well, gotta go. Got night court at the Carousel tonight, and it'll be cranking up after awhile. The police, they told me we should have a brand new, fresh batch of defendants coming, some of them ready for the picking." He winked and rubbed his palms together. "Some are out-of-towners, they say."

Smudge opened the door and hurried out, leaving me with a feeling of guilt and unable to say anything by way of apology or explanation to Dixie, especially with Billy Joe sitting right there, grinning like a possum with a belly full of persimmons.

After Smudge cleared out and Billy Joe sat back down, he motioned for Dixie and me to sit also. It had been a long time since I'd seen him as happy as he appeared to be right then, and I knew why. Whatever progress I'd made with Dixie while traveling with her, it had now been stopped dead in its tracks, if not completely reversed.

"Deloris," Billy Joe said, talking like nothing in the world had happened right then, "how about if I draft a motion for summary judgment and an affidavit from you to go with it. That oughtta get things rolling. Okay? I'd kinda like to file it with our answer to the complaint."

"Fine with me," I said, not really thinking about it. "One thing, before I forget. That fella Turbyfill—"

"What about him?" Billy Joe said.

"You might check this out, but I believe he's got a criminal record. Nothing major, though. Also, he's a little slow."

"You and him, y'all not kin, are you?" He winked at Dixie and laughed. She didn't laugh back. Neither did I.

A silence then fell upon the room, broken only when Billy Joe laughed again—a nervous kind of one. He stood and nodded at Dixie. "After Deloris leaves here in a few minutes, how about getting me my form book and plan on working late this evening. All right? I need a form to go by when I draft his affidavit and the motion."

Then it hit me. Billy Joe had suckered me into a way for him to be alone with Dixie that evening. I suspected he wanted to keep me away from her.

"Don't you want me to stay and help you with all that, Billy Joe?" I asked, hoping to put a dent into Billy Joe's scheming. "I don't mind. I don't have anything else to do."

"Oh, I wouldn't think of doing that to you. Won't be much to it. Besides, you're more of a witness and a party here than a lawyer. So, I think it best you not participate in the legal stuff. You know what they say, *A lawyer who represents himself has a fool for a client.* " Billy Joe laughed. "You don't wanna prove the truth of that statement, do you?"

I sensed my face heat up, but I didn't say anything. I really didn't have any choice right then other than to put up with him and his smart mouth.

He went on. "Anyway, Dixie is familiar with the file you sent by her this morning—that shoebox material and other stuff—the outline, that'll help a lot. So, you just head on home. Rest up some. Get you a good night's sleep. We'll take care of everything. Won't we, Dixie?"

"No question about it," she said through clenched teeth.

I didn't want to leave, not with Dixie being left alone with him and her acting like she was mad at me. I wanted to explain to her about my visit to Smudge's office and try to get her to understand I didn't mean anything by looking at Mavis the way Smudge said I did—and anyway, even if I did, it was just a natural thing for a man to do.

"But, Billy Joe, won't that be a waste of time—filing a motion like that?" I asked, hoping to change his mind. "Judge Nunamaker," I said, referring to the probate judge, "she's never in her life given anybody a summary judgment. She told me one time, *There're four things I don't believe in: Santa Claus, the Easter Bunny, the Tooth Fairy, and granting summary judgment.* She says a motion like that is a complete waste of time. And I think she's right because you can't appeal from an order denying one. I learned that the hard way. I tried it one time, doncha know."

"Well, maybe for Judge Nunamaker this'll be a waste of time," Billy Joe said, "but not for me. I'd like to use the motion to kinda smoke old Smudge out—to find out some more about what his eye witness is gonna say happened when Loomis executed his will. Smudge'll have to have him give an affidavit if for no other reason than to fight your affidavit, so to speak. Another thing, when we have the hearing on the motion, Smudge'll probably run his mouth and tell us everything we need to know about his case—his legal theories and so forth—that is, if he's got any legal theories, which I seriously doubt."

I could see I wasn't about to dissuade Billy Joe from going ahead with preparing the motion. So, I gave up trying. "I'll say this. Whatever Turbyfill says, I guarantee it's gonna be words somebody else put in his mouth. And when we do reach trial, it won't be nothing but a swearing contest—"

Billy Joe pushed back in his chair, leaned way back, and crossed his legs. "And that's exactly why I wanna make the motion, don't you see? Like I say, after the hearing on the motion, we'll know better what Turbyfill'll supposedly testify to at trial. Even better, we'll pretty much have his testimony locked in by his affidavit. I'll then be better able to get myself prepared for his cross-examination, doncha see."

What Billy Joe didn't say is that my own affidavit would "pretty much" restrict my own testimony as well and would enable Smudge to prepare his cross-examination of me a whole lot better too. Our saving grace, if there be one, would be that Smudge never prepared for court and always flew by the seat of his pants.

Billy Joe glanced at Dixie and wiped a hand across his mouth. "Hmmmm, Deloris. You know what? You do raise an interesting question. Who will the jury believe between the two of you?"

Billy Joe dropped his chin into his hand, his elbow resting on the arm of the chair. "Let's see here. Let me think about all that's happened here lately with you. And mind you, these are things you yourself disclosed to me, some stuff I heard about for the first time this very day. And a few things Dixie'd told me about."

After a moment, he removed his hand and stood to address an imaginary jury.

"The basic question you will be asked to decide, members of the jury, is this: *Do you believe the testimony of a dim-wit with a minor criminal record, or do you believe the testimony of a lawyer who twice flunked the bar; a lawyer who practices out of a used milk truck and doesn't even have a telephone of his own; a lawyer who gives away cold water to attract clients; a lawyer who gets chased from a church by the family and friends of the lawyer's own client who are there mourning and attending the client's funeral; a lawyer who, because she has to go to the ladies' room, abandons a beautiful woman in a place she has never been to in her life and has neither family nor friends to turn to for help; a lawyer who takes up with a couple of vagabond show folks, one of who's dummy purportedly gets saved at a tent revival and turns to preaching to little children, no less; a lawyer who, after being struck down by the dislocated head of another dummy, gets his rear end whipped in a juke joint by a prostitute and her pimp, no less; a lawyer who is himself accused by the police of being a pimp but who manages somehow to get himself off on a technicality—a technicality, mind you; a lawyer whose roommate gets shot on a dance floor—note that I said a dance floor—a dance floor in a durn honky-tonk, of all places; a lawyer who sets in motion events that led to a war hero's beloved, sweet little puppy probably being shot and killed, and—now get this—a lawyer whose first and middle names are names usually given to girls?*

He leaned toward me. "Now, if you ask me, that's gonna be a tough question for any jury to decide."

Dixie also put her two cents worth in. "And don't forget about the sex fiend he got off scot-free before we even left the state. Folks sure won't like that when they hear about it."

I couldn't believe my own ears. "I got off? You the one really did it, Dixie. You know that."

Dixie pointed to herself. "Me? I wasn't his lawyer."

Billy Joe smiled. "Oh, well. If you'll excuse us, Deloris, Dixie and me, we've got work to do. Trust me on this."

I left them alone and went on home feeling very unhappy about how things had worked out for me.

CHAPTER FOURTEEN

On the morning the court scheduled a hearing on Billy Joe's motion for summary judgment, I met Roda Anne Harrison and her husband at the Trailways bus station and whisked them in my truck to the courthouse.

We met Billy Joe and Dixie out front. Dixie mumbled a good morning to me but greeted the Harrisons with the enthusiasm a person ordinarily reserves for a lost child. Still, I had to give it to Dixie: were it not for her imagination when we searched the public records in Abilene, none of this would have been happening right then.

Billy Joe played the gentleman to the hilt, being polite in every way. He even apologized to them about their mode of transportation from the bus station to the courthouse, attempting to be funny as he did it and embarrassing me in the process. "You know why Deloris chose to put his office in a milk truck, don't you?"

The Harrisons offered him blank faces and shook their heads.

Billy Joe laughed. "Well, he figured if it turned out he couldn't make it as a lawyer he could always use it to make milk runs."

Neither Roda Anne nor her husband laughed. I certainly didn't. As for Dixie, she didn't laugh either. She bit her lips and closed her eyes. When she opened them, she looked straight at me and shook her head. That was the first mark of kindness she'd shown me since Smudge opened his big mouth and suggested I had lusted after his secretary—which I didn't do. Well, maybe I did a little.

Billy Joe cleared his throat, his face a little pink, "I think it's time we get ourselves inside. Mrs. Harrison, I guess Deloris has already briefed y'all on what's gonna happen this morning?"

"No, sir," Roda Anne said. She glanced at me, appearing concerned.

Billy Joe peered at me like he couldn't believe his ears.

I threw up my hands. "Don't look at me," I said. "You're the one handling the litigation."

When we reached the courthouse portico, Billy Joe signaled for everyone to stop. He used the opportunity to explain the purpose of the hearing, showing off as he did it by using a lot of legal jargon. The way in which the Harrisons received his elaborate explanation led me to believe they didn't understand a single word of it.

We took the elevator up to the third-floor courtroom used by the probate court for its hearings. The instant we exited the elevator and entered the hallway we encountered Bessie Phillips and her brothers. They gave us their backs and made a beeline for the courtroom with Heckle and Jeckle tussling with each other to see which one could get through the door first.

We waited until the Phillipses settled into their seats before we went in. As we waited, Smudge Chiselbrook came running up the stairs at the end of the hall. He appeared out of breath. His hand held a single, flat-looking file folder. I speculated that, if it held anything, it would be a grocery list with Miller High Life Beer heading the list.

"Hey, Deloris, Billy Joe," he said, all in a pant. "Y'all seen my folks? Know if they're here yet?" He paused long enough to catch his breath. "Whew. Man. Whooooo-we. Scared I wouldn't make it. Whew. Been at the Carousel. Landed two cases. Well, one really. Other fella, he kept telling me he was innocent and wanting a trial. Know what I did? I give him back his five bucks and told him to go try it his own self. Hated doing that. Five dollars is five dollars. Innocent, my foot. Whew."

"Your clients just got here. They're inside," Billy Joe said, gesturing toward the courtroom door.

"They are? Good," he said, and away he flew.

Billy Joe turned to me. "I meant to tell you, Deloris, but Judge Nunamaker disqualified herself in this case. The chief justice assigned another judge in her place."

"Why'd she do that?" I asked.

"Way I understand it, she disqualified herself because she and Miss Phillips, they are in some kinda women's organization together—or something like that. I'm not sure."

"And who'd the chief justice send?"

"Judge Leon Askew. He's fairly new. He practiced here in the Low Country. Mainly probate work, title searches, and property closings. That sort of thing. He married a Fraser from Charleston. He's the one who ran against old Judge Ravenel a year or so ago. Beat him in the primary."

Billy Joe went on to tell me that he'd learned Judge Askew enjoyed the respect of his county bar but not as much as Judge Nunamaker did with ours. Judge Askew couched much of what he said and did in baseball terms. One of his favorite lines, Billy Joe understood, was "Only in baseball can you go home again." And it was said he adored the St. Louis Cardinals. If a lawyer so much as even looked like he pulled for any team other than the Cardinals, it was Katy bar the door for that lawyer. Whoever Billy Joe talked to also advised him to make sure he referred to a Cardinal great sometime during argument. He said the judge would beam like a London searchlight whenever a lawyer did that.

We walked into the courtroom. Billy Joe and I bid a good morning to the deputy clerk of court who sat at a desk below the judge's bench. I took a seat next to Billy Joe at one of the two counsel tables. Dixie and the Harrisons sat right behind us inside the bar. To our right at the other table sat Smudge and Bessie. In the meantime, the two brothers selected places on the first row of the bench seats in the spectator section. I surmised Bessie didn't want them within the well of the courtroom, fearing they might detract from her self-appointed importance.

At ten o'clock, Judge Askew, a gangly, middle-age fella with a full head of hair, jogged through a side door, bounded up the steps, and onto the bench platform. His entry reminded me of a home team taking the field. A tall, elderly man with a mournful face best suited for a funeral parlor rather than a courtroom and outfitted in a black coat and large badge followed. He stationed himself at the door, his arms crossed in front. I presumed him to be the judge's bailiff.

Judge Askew wasted no time in throwing his first pitch. "Good morning, ladies and gentlemen," he said, putting on glasses. "All right, this contest is between Bessie Phillips and her brothers, who are represented by Oleander Chiselbrook, Esquire, and Deloris Ursel Meek, who manages a decedent's estate. Let's see, it's the Estate of William Howard Taft Loomis. Representing the latter is Billy Joe Pratt, Esquire."

The judge looked up. "Is Miss Meek with us?" His eyes landed on Dixie. "Are you she, Miss?"

Dixie stood just as Billy Joe pushed his chair back to do likewise.

They both spoke at the same time, but Billy Joe deferred to Dixie after his first couple of words.

"Your Honor, Deloris Ursel is seated by Mr. Pratt. And he's a man."

The judge peeked down at me and then at the papers on his desk. "Score an error for me. Yes, the caption does read 'Executor' not 'Executrix'. Sorry about that, Mr. Meek. I meant no disrespect. Excuse me a moment." He looked around. "Linwood? Oh, Linwood."

The man in the black coat rushed to the bench steps. "Yes, sir, Your Honor."

"I left my fountain pen on my desk in yonder. Please fetch it for me."

Linwood rushed away, as if he was stealing second base.

Judge Askew adjusted his tie. "All right, gentlemen, let's play ball. Mr. Pratt batter up."

Billy Joe stood to begin as Linwood returned, fountain pen in hand. He waited until Linwood resumed his post at the door before he began his argument. "Your Honor, I ask you to look at the file which contains a will that is signed by the testator, dated, and witnessed by three witnesses. In the will, the testator, Colonel William Howard Taft Loomis, leaves all of his estate, all of his real and personal property to one Roda Anne Harrison. The file also contains a certified copy of a birth certificate, which shows Colonel Loomis to be the father of Roda Anne Loomis, now Roda Anne Harrison, according to Mrs. Harrison's affidavit, also of record. There is in the file you have there a certified copy of a divorce decree where the judge makes a finding that Roda Anne is Colonel Loomis' daughter. Finally, there is an affidavit from Deloris Meek which states there wasn't any undue influence or coercion or threats made against the colonel when he executed his will.

"I would think, Your Honor, that with his affidavit and the presumption of—I forget what it's called—"

"Strike one, Mr. Pratt," the judge called out, raising his fist.

"Sir?"

"Play ball."

"Anyway, it's when everything looks in line. You know, as it should be. Least on its face, it does. I wish I could remember the word."

The judge rubbed his mouth. "You not trying to throw me some kind of curve ball here, are you, Mr. Pratt. Because if you are, I'll call you out right fast like."

Billy Joe's Adam's apple rose and fell. "No, sir."

"You won't get to first base with that argument, sir," the judge said. He turned toward the side. "Linwood, oh Linwood."

Linwood took a couple of steps toward the bench while repeatedly striking his left palm with his right fist over and over again. "Yes, Your Honor."

"I need the copy of *American Jurisprudence* that discusses wills and whatnot."

The bailiff looked confused. "Whatnot, Judge?"

The judge frowned. "Linwood, when I pitch 'em to you, you gotta catch 'em. It's one of those green books on the shelf there by the coffee pot. One that says 'Wills' on the spine."

"Tell you what, Mr. Pratt, I'm calling you out. The top half of the inning is over. It's the other side's time to see if they can hit the ball." He looked at Smudge. "Mr. Chiselbrook, is it?"

Smudge jumped to his feet. "Yes, sir."

"All right, grab you a bat and take your swings."

"Thank you, Judge." Smudge took a couple steps around his table, stationing himself to the judge's left, directly in front of Billy Joe. "I had a wise old lawyer tell me one time, when the judge seems to be going your way, best to step aside and let him take his swings. But I gotta tell you, though, I disagree with Your Honor on one point."

The judge's mouth flew open and his glasses dropped down on his nose as he stared at Smudge over them. "What's that, sir?"

"You say he throwed you a curve ball. No, sir. It was more like a spit ball."

The judge pushed back his glasses, smiled, and tipped back in his chair.

Linwood returned with the legal encyclopedia and held it up to the judge. The judge motioned for Linwood to bring the book forward and then reached out for it as he drew near.

"Yes, sir, he threw you a spit ball. But lemme say something here, Your Honor. Stan Musial, that great Cardinal, was quoted one time as saying something like this: *Whenever anybody throws you a spitball, the thing you do is try to hit it on the dry side.* That's what—"

Judge Askew interrupted. "Stan Musial said that, you say?"

"Yes, sir. Well, something along those lines. That's not no exact quote."

"Give me a second while I write that down. I'd never heard that before."

Smudge waited for the judge to look up from his desk before continuing, his lips stretched into a huge grin. I gathered he thought he had hit a grand slam.

"What I'm gonna try to do here, if Your Honor please, is try and follow the advice of Stan the Man. I'm gonna try and hit the dry side. How does Mr. Pratt throw a spitball? He does that by not mentioning we'd filed an affidavit a while ago of a witness to the will who seen what happened when the colonel wrote his name down on the thing Mr. Meek'd done drawed up for him. Look there in the file, Judge. It's that one signed by a gentleman named Jerome Turbyfill."

The judge withdrew a document from the case file and gave it a quick check.

Smudge continued on. "Look there what he said, Judge. Turbyfill said him and Mr. Jay Wyndam and some other fella, they were told to come in the house there by Mr. Meek. They'd been outside doing some work, panting or something other. They said before he called them in, they heard all this yelling going on inside the house while they were standing there by the back steps. They come in the house, and they said Colonel Loomis was sitting at the kitchen table, crying and shaking his head and kept saying over and over, *I don't wanna do this. How come you making me do this?* and Mr. Meek, he kept yelling something, best he recalled, something what sounded like, *You'll go to Hell or jail if you don't,* he wasn't sure which. But he did tell the colonel *You better do as I tell you to, or else* and shook his fist at him a time or two. After that, the colonel signed on the line where Mr. Meek told him to. The three witnesses, they did too, and then they went on back outside, leaving the colonel in there, just a'crying. Turbyfill also says—"

The judge motioned for Smudge to stop. "Where are the other two witnesses?"

Smudge turned his head and glanced at Billy Joe before answering Judge Askew. "In baseball terminology, Your Honor, Wyndam's been traded. He's now on another team, hopefully one higher up—you know, in the major leagues." Smudge raised his eyes toward the ceiling and placed a hand over his heart.

The judge smiled. "I'm with you. And the other one?"

Smudge shook his head. "He's left the ballpark and gone on to parts unknown, Judge, Your Honor."

Again the judge turned to his right. "Linwood, oh Linwood. Now, I need the code book. Get the one with the probate code in it. You know which one."

"So, Your Honor, Mr. Pratt's got Mr. Meek's affidavit, which he says everything was hokie-dokie, and I got an affidavit which says no it wasn't neither. What that means is, way I remember them telling us in law school, is you can't give them no summary judgment. There's a conflict here in the evidence. We gotta have a trial, Your Honor. A jury's gotta decide this. If there's one thing I remember about what they tried to teach us at law school, it's that. Am I mistaken about this, sir?"

It surprised me that Smudge remembered he even went to law school, much less that he remembered something they taught there.

Linwood returned with the code book and handed it up to the judge. As Smudge continued to stand, Judge Askew leafed through the code, pausing every now and then at one page and then another. Two or three minutes went by before the judge said anything more.

"Mr. Chiselbrook?"

"Yes, sir, Your Honor?"

"You ever heard of the Statute on Descent and Distribution?"

Smudge appeared caught napping at first base for a couple of seconds. "Oh, yes, sir. That's the main reason for how come we sued. That's what we want. We want a decent distribution of the colonel's property. All they offered us was an old used Chrysler automobile. Now, that's not no decent distribution, I don't care what anybody says.

"My clients, they feel like, Your Honor, they're entitled to a decent distribution, and by that we mean a fair one, like half the property—at least that much. We think because Miss Phillips and her brothers over there, because they were the niece and nephews of the colonel's late wife, the one who left the colonel all that property to begin with, it's not fair for every bit of it to go beyond the blood line of the original owner. Why, if that happened she'd turn over in her grave.

So, yeah, we want a decent distribution. I appreciate you calling that to my attention, Judge. I'd plumb forgot about it. I reckon I was too busy concentrating on hitting that spit ball Mr. Pratt threw at me. So, like that old lawyer told me to do, I'm just gonna get outta your way and let you come on through and pinch-hit for me, Your Honor. Much obliged." He turned to go back to his counsel table.

"Before you sit down, Mr. Chiselbrook, I must point out to you I'm not a player."

Smudge ducked his head. "No, sir."

"I'm an umpire."

"Yes, sir."

Smudge retreated to his counsel table and sat down, his shoulders slumped.

The judge shifted around in his chair and sat up straight.

"Mr. Chiselbrook, sir, you rounded third and you headed for home plate, but I'm afraid, sir, you didn't quite make it there. Nope, you didn't. I'm sorry but you were cut off from left field."

Smudge stood. "From left field? Uh, I'm not sure I follow you, Your Honor."

"It's very simple, Mr. Chiselbrook, you're out. Nowhere do I find any roster that lists the Phillipses on the colonel's team or, in other words, as blood relatives of the late Colonel Loomis. You seem to concede as much in your remarks.

"But I do find a roster of his that lists Roda Anne Harrison, formerly Roda Anne Loomis. In fact, she is the only player listed there. And under the Statute of Descent and Distribution of this State, she alone is his sole heir and legatee. And by the way, sir, its 'descent and distribution,' not 'decent distribution.' "

Smudge, still standing, said, "I don't follow you, Your Honor. I mean, what about my witness, Mr. Turbyfill and what he said happened? Don't that count?"

The judge smiled down upon Smudge like a benevolent father about to teach a wayward son one of life's lessons. "It's sorta like a foul ball on a third strike, Mr. Chiselbrook. It often doesn't matter all that much in the final analysis. You see, sir, even if I were able to uphold your claim that Mr. Meek exercised undue influence or applied coercion to get the colonel to sign or execute the will, you still lose because the next pitch strikes you out. That's because, if the colonel died intestate—that is, without a will—Mrs. Harrison would still inherit all his property under the Statute of Descent and Distribution. Apparently, she is his lone relative—his lone heir under the law."

Smudge took a peek at Bessie Phillips next to him. She looked white as a sheet. Her lips had begun to quiver and her shoulders shake.

"In a nutshell, Mr. Chiselbrook, the game is over. Score? One to nothing. I see absolutely no reason for the court to entertain this suit any further. You would lose in the end, Mr. Chiselbrook. So, I'm not allowing this contest to go into extra innings. See no need in it. It'd be a waste of time for the court, for you and Mr. Pratt, and for the players, the Phillipses and the Executor of the Loomis Estate, Mr. Meek. Summary judgment in favor of the estate."

"But, Your Honor," Smudge said, sputtering, "you've done thrown me kind of fastball here. So fast, I didn't even see it coming, if you wanna know the truth."

"In this game, Counsel, you gotta be ready for whatever is thrown your way. A veteran like you ought to know that. You're no rookie."

Smudge managed a laugh. "Well, Your Honor, how could I have been ready for it? I didn't have no way of knowing that was gonna be an issue I had to deal with this morning—that statute, I mean. So, I guess what I'm trying to tell Your Honor is I plead—what do they call it?—the 'Doctrine of Unthinkability.' Yeah, the 'Doctrine of Unthinkability.' That's cause I didn't even think about it."

"But Mr. Chiselbrook," the judge said, leaning forward, "while you didn't think about the statute, I did. Therefore, the doctrine, if there really is such a thing—which I seriously doubt—it would not be applicable here, now would it?"

Smudge nodded toward Bessie Phillips and took a deep breath. "No, sir. I don't reckon so. But still, I think you oughtta at least give me a chance to take a good swing at whatcha threw me. Not for me, but for these good folks here, Miss Phillips and her two brothers."

Judge Askew jerked his thumb over his right shoulder. "Mr. Chiselbrook, you, sir, have been called out. Again, the game's over."

At that, Bessie jumped to her feet and leveled an angry finger at the judge. "Is that all this is to you, sir? Some kind of stupid game?"

Smudge turned to quiet her, but she would have none of it. She brushed away his hand and scowled at him so I could almost swear I saw Smudge tremble.

As for the judge, he simply sat back in his chair, folded his hands beneath his chin as in prayer, put on a blank face, and let Bessie have at him. I didn't time her, but she must've gone on for about ten minutes haranguing the judge about how unfair he was and how he had condoned the stealing of property rightfully theirs in ruling the way he did. All the while, Smudge sat with his head buried in his hands, shaking it from side to side and muttering something I couldn't quite make out.

When Bessie declared, "that's all I've got to say," the judge smiled and motioned to the court reporter. "Madam Court Reporter," he said, "let the record reflect I'm awarding attorney fees and costs to the estate. Better yet, I'm awarding double costs. Get me up an affidavit of the expenses and your time, Mr. Pratt, including the last ten minutes or so."

* * * * *

We left the courthouse and headed on foot to Billy Joe's office nearby. Despite the wind and the threat of rain, I walked with a spring in my step.

Billy Joe talked about himself all the way back and bragged about the fine job he did in representing the estate. Yet the truth of the matter is Billy Joe didn't win the case. The probate judge won it for him. The alternative argument about the Statute of Descent and Distribution originated with him, not with Billy Joe. Still, though, he did put together the record that included all the documents necessary to sustain the ground on which the court could uphold the colonel's wish to leave all of his estate to his daughter.

Before Billy Joe and I joined all the others in his private office, I drew him to one side. "Hold up a second, Billy Joe. Don't go in there right yet," I said, "I wanna ask you something."

"Yeah? What?" He spoke like he was in a big hurry.

"You reckon," I said in a hushed tone, "Roda Anne really is the colonel's daughter?"

Billy Joe arched his shoulders. "Who the hell knows?" he whispered back. "Anyway, the law says she is, and that settles that as far as I'm concerned." He inclined his head in the direction of the door. "Come on, let's go. Everybody's waiting on us."

As soon as we walked into the office, the Harrisons again congratulated Billy Joe on his victory and thanked him. Billy Joe just beamed.

I congratulated him as well and instructed him in the Harrison's presence to submit his bill as soon as possible, if his attorney fees exceeded what the court ordered the Phillipses to pay. I pointed out that I wanted to get all the colonel's bills satisfied and to do everything else necessary to close the estate so that the Harrisons could get on with their lives. They had indicated to me earlier that morning they wanted to relocate to our community in the event the probate court upheld the colonel's will.

I said my goodbyes to the Harrisons and prepared to leave.

Before I could go, Dixie said to me, "Wait up, Deloris, I'll walk out with you."

I can't tell you how much that floored me, it took me so aback.

Billy Joe looked absolutely mortified, standing there with his mouth hanging open and his eyes blinking.

Once outside, Dixie took hold of my hand and said to me, "Deloris, I want you to know I'm sorry for the way I've been treating you since Smudge came by the office that day. It was wrong for me to fault you like I did, especially since she probably encouraged you to look at her the way he said you did."

I started to say something, but she shushed me by touching my lips with her fingertips.

"What say tonight you and me go to dinner at some nice, quiet restaurant to celebrate your victory and then take in a movie? Want to?"

I looked toward the front door of the office building, expecting Billy Joe to come bursting through it at any moment. "What about him in yonder?"

"What about him? I just work for him, that's all."

Then she stood on her tiptoes and kissed me right smack on my lips.

"You know what?" she said, stepping back. "Your parents did right in naming you 'Ursel.' You are a bear—a big old teddy bear."

I reached for Dixie to put my arms around her, intending to return the kiss. But before I could do so, a car screeched to a stop to my right, attracting my attention. Dixie and I both turned toward the sound and watched as the right-rear door of a taxicab flew open.

And who should jump out and race toward me, her high heels clicking as she ran? None other than Ginger Childree, that's who.

"Deloris! Deloris!" she cried.

Without so much as a glance at Dixie, Ginger threw her arms about my neck and hugged me. "Oh, I'm so glad I found you. I called the number on your business card. They told me I might find you here or at the courthouse, one."

I looked over at Dixie who, with her arms crossed and her body rocking to and fro, stood staring squint-eyed at Ginger and me. My face, already burning with embarrassment, burned hotter still.

Ginger began to sob. "You've gotta help me, Deloris. You just gotta. Kuddles . . . Kuddles, she's—"

"What about Kuddles?"

"After we got through taking the tent down in Winston-Salem and packing up to go to Wilmington, the next thing I know. . . "

"Yes," I said, separating myself from her.

"She's run off with Brother Holcomb."

ABOUT THE AUTHOR

Bert Goolsby is a former Chief Deputy Attorney General of South Carolina and a former Judge of the South Carolina Court of Appeals. A native of Alabama, having been raised in Dothan, he and his wife the former Mary Ellen "Prue" Fraser of Walterboro, South Carolina, make their home in Columbia. He earned an undergraduate degree at The Citadel, a law degree at the University of South Carolina, and an advanced law degree at the University of Virginia.

www.ingramcontent.com/pod-product-compliance
Lightning Source LLC
Chambersburg PA
CBHW071529220526
45469CB00003B/696